Phyllis Grzegzka, SSND

D1125690

FIDELITY:

ISSUES OF EMOTIONAL LIVING
IN AN AGE OF STRESS
FOR CLERGY AND RELIGIOUS

FIDELITY:

ISSUES OF EMOTIONAL LIVING
IN AN AGE OF STRESS
FOR CLERGY AND RELIGIOUS

THE SIXTH
PSYCHOTHEOLOGICAL SYMPOSIUM

SEAN D. SAMMON

RITA ZEIS

BERNARD J. BUSH

AUDREY E. CAMPBELL-WRAY

VINCENT M. BILOTTA III

KATHLEEN E. KELLEY

J. WILLIAM HUBER

EDITED BY JOSEPH L. HART

WITH A FOREWORD BY THOMAS A. KANE

AFFIRMATION BOOKS
WHITINSVILLE, MASSACHUSETTS

Published with Ecclesiastical Permission

First Edition

©1981 by House of Affirmation, Inc.

All rights reserved, including the right of reproduction in whole or in part, in any form or by any means, electronic or mechanical, including photocopying, or by any information storage and retrieval systems, without permission in writing from the publisher. Inquiries should be addressed to Editor, Affirmation Books, 456 Hill Street, Whitinsville, MA 01588.

Library of Congress Cataloging in Publication Data
Psychotheological Symposium, 6th, Fontbonne Academy, etc., 1980.
    Fidelity: issues of emotional living in an age of stress for clergy and religious.
    Includes bibliographical references.
    1. Catholic Church—Clergy—Psychology—Congresses.
2. Monastic and religious life—Psychology—Congresses.
3. Commitment (Psychology)—Congresses. I. Sammon, Sean D., 1947- . II. Hart, Joseph E. II. Title.
IV. Title: Issues of emotional living in an age of stress for clergy and religious.
BX1912.P79   1980   248.8'9   81-533

ISBN 0-89571-011-0   AACR2

Printed by
Mercantile Printing Company, Worcester, Massachusetts
United States of America

To

present and former residents

of the House of Affirmation

with love and gratitude

All income derived from the sale of this book is used to provide care for priests and religious suffering from emotional unrest.

AFFIRMATION BOOKS is an important part of the ministry of the House of Affirmation, International Therapeutic Center for Clergy and Religious, founded by Sister Anna Polcino, S.C.M.M., M.D.

CONTENTS

FOREWORD

When people marry, they say "until death do us part." Still, two out of three marriages end in divorce. Often people make final vows and then want to leave the religious life a few years later. A man is ordained a priest forever, yet it is not uncommon to hear of men asking for laicization after five, ten, or fifteen years. There is a lot of discussion about temporary commitment, the meaninglessness of permanent choice, and the so-called absurdity of pledging or of expecting fidelity.

We all need to think about and to talk and listen to one another concerning the reality and meaning of fidelity. I have heard religious and priests pray that the Lord might be merciful to those who have abandoned their marriage or religious vows. Yet I have observed some of these same people who have "stayed with it" being apparently seriously unfaithful to their commitment, and lacking integrity in radiating the warm charity of Christ. It is not for us to judge people or to brand them with infidelity. Rather, we need to raise the question of fidelity and reflect on it with other Christians. This reasoning is behind the publication of the essays in this volume.

When we reflect on the gospels we learn that there is an important place for fidelity, lifelong fidelity, in marriage, priesthood, and religious life. But fidelity makes sense only when there are life-giving relationships with Christ, others, self, and our world! To be faithful to commitments to relationships is to embrace not only moments of joy, but also the inevitable realities of tragedy and ambiguity. Adult living is difficult work, and fidelity to relationships is possible only for adults gifted and cooperating with divine grace. "Love demands effort and personal commitment to the will of God. It means discipline and sacrifice, but also it means joy and human fulfillment," Pope John Paul II told us in New York City in October, 1979.

This present book, *Fidelity: Issues of Emotional Living in an Age of Stress for Clergy and Religious* offers a group of essays that are not intended to be conclusive statements, but rather instruments to encourage the reader to further personal reflection and academic investigation of the subject matter. When we consider fidelity with regard to Christian marriage, priesthood, and religious life, we are not merely reflecting on patterns of human behavior, but operations of divine grace. Therefore, some aspects of fidelity will always lie beyond our understanding.

Father Joseph L. Hart, S.S.E., Ph.D., editor of this volume, is director of our House of Affirmation in Whitinsville, Massachusetts. At this residential center, Father Hart has as his mandate to preserve fidelity to spiritual values and to guide the scientific concerns of our House of Affirmation psychotheological residential therapeutic community. Signficantly, Father Hart has the task of editing this volume as he celebrates his twenty-fifth anniversary of ordination to the priesthood.

Once again, Affirmation Books is happy to present you, our readers, with a new volume to challenge your thought and encourage your faith.

Thomas A. Kane, Ph.D., D.P.S.

Priest, Diocese of Worcester
Publisher, Affirmation Books
Whitinsville, Massachusetts

January 6, 1981

PREFACE

Carl Jung reportedly was one day seated on a train departing from the Zurich *Bahnhof*. The conductor benignly observed the 84-year old master of analytic psychology going through his briefcase in a vain search for his ticket.

Jung was well known to the Swiss conductor, so the genial official reassured his famous passenger.

"Herr Doctor will find his ticket after the journey, and will mail it to the railroad office."

Jung immediately sat up, and replied with spirit: "All well and good, my friend, but the problem is not the missing ticket. The problem is, where am I going?"[1]

"Where am I going?" a question each of us must ask ourselves over and over again in our reflective moments, is one that serves as a stimulus for symposiums sponsored by the House of Affirmation. In these days of stress and uncertainty, "where am I going?" is a question asked by many of us. However, it needs an individual response from each person, a satisfactory answer for the one asking it—until the individual is ready to ask the question again. Which of us could cast the first stone at Jung?

---

1. *Voices* 15 (Fall, 1979): 44.

For six successive years the House of Affirmation staff has presented symposiums on significant topics in a manner intended to help individuals work out their answers to such questions. We do not pretend to give answers, but rather do we strive to provide reflections and challenges which individuals can use to create their own directions, to determine for themselves where they are going. We have addressed the issues holistically by using the best insights provided by reputable contemporary psychology accompanied by appropriate reflections from theology, religion, and scripture, and we integrate these disciplines where possible.

The theme of the sixth annual symposium was fidelity, a subject that provided our speakers with a unique opportunity and challenge. As trained psychologists they were asked to address issues that are an integral part of religious and theological systems. The reader will find in the pages of this volume that the speakers dealt forthrightly with such thorny issues as value systems, religious commitments, and personal standards. Their papers are in the tradition of Viktor Frankl who was among the first to demonstrate the appropriateness of using psychology and psychiatry to deal with these questions. Frankl, a psychiatrist who survived Nazi concentration camps, has shown how much our emotional health and well-being depend on the *meaningfulness* we find or create and put into our lives.[2] Fidelity to ourselves and to those externals that have meaning for our lives is also necessary for our psychological peace of mind. It is to these issues that the

2. Viktor E. Frankl, *Man's Search for Meaning* (Boston: Beacon Press, 1962).

symposium speakers addressed themselves, and with a sense of pride we present their papers in this volume. Their insights will help us create our own answers to the question: "Where am I going?" In addition, Reverend J. William Huber, assistant director of our Webster Groves center, kindly prepared for this volume an article that complements the speakers' contributions.

As I now express gratitude to all who presented papers at the Boston, San Francisco, and St. Louis sessions of the 1980 symposium, I would also like to thank the audiences who attended the sessions. During each year they stimulate us indirectly as we consider what theme to address at the symposium, and how to develop the topics in a way that helps all who attend. So, although members of the audience are physically present with us a mere seven hours of one day, they are spiritually present to us throughout the year, inspiring our best efforts as we prepare for this annual and important event.

The symposium sessions could not have been held without a large supporting group of friends and staff members who donated their time and energies on the days involved: to each and all, we offer heartfelt gratitude. We are also grateful to those who extended hospitality for the meetings: the Sisters of St. Joseph at Fontbonne Academy in Milton, the Sisters of the Presentation in San Francisco, and the staff at St. John's Mercy Hospital in St. Louis. Others who helped to make the symposium days successful were members of the reactor panels, and those who joined me in moderating the meetings: Reverend Bernard Bush in San Francisco and Sister Kathleen Kelley in St. Louis.

At each of our centers, the symposium is one day of an Affirmation Weekend when many former residents return to renew friendships and to recall their experiences at the House of Affirmation. Their presence reanimates our dedication to our own goals and purposes. We thank them for this contribution as we thank our present residents who give this therapeutic community its reason for being.

Rev. Joseph L. Hart, S.S.E.
House of Affirmation
Whitinsville, Massachusetts

Brother Sean D. Sammon, F.M.S., M.A., is a full-time psychotherapist at the House of Affirmation in Whitinsville, Massachusetts. A member of the Marist Brothers of the Schools since 1966, Brother Sammon received his undergraduate education at Marist College, Poughkeepsie, New York. He did graduate work in psychology at the New School for Social Research in New York City and is currently a candidate for a doctoral degree in clinical psychology at Fordham University. Before joining the staff of the House of Affirmation, Brother Sammon interned in clinical psychology at St. Barnabas Hospital, New York, the Franklin D. Roosevelt Veterans Administration Hospital, New York, and The Institute of Living in Hartford, Connecticut. He is an associate member of the American Psychological Association, the Scientific Research Society of North America, and Psychologists Interested in Religious Issues. His research interests include the adult development of American religious, and the fields of neuropsychology and alcoholism.

THE MEANING OF "MEANING IT"

Sean D. Sammon

"Something must have happened to me sometime," Bobby Slocum warns us at the outset of Joseph Heller's narrative of midlife turmoil, "something happened to me that robbed me of confidence and courage and left me with a fear of discovery and a positive dread of everything unknown that may occur."[1]

Midway through the journey of his life, Slocum confesses that he gets the "willies" when he sees a closed door. He imagines something horrible is happening behind it, something that will affect him adversely. His hands perspire. His voice sounds strange. His wife and children are unhappy in their separate ways. He wonders why.

A careful examination of Slocum's life, his choices regarding work, marriage, and family, and his values and interests provides a partial answer to his puzzled musings.

---

1. Joseph Heller, *Something Happened* (New York: Ballantine Books, 1975), p. 6.

Simply stated, Slocum has ceased to practice the virtue of fidelity. He has failed on two counts: one, not giving prominence in his life to his *dream;* and two, refusing to allow others any claim over himself.

One's dream answers the question, "What shall I do with my adult life?" in a way which gives the individual an opportunity for personal fulfillment. To live in harmony with one's dream implies a life of integrity, while betrayal of one's dream leads to an impoverished existence. In addition, yielding to another some claim over one's life forces a man or woman to face the question of intimacy: "Am I sure enough of myself to risk being influenced through this close relationship?" An affirmative answer to this question of intimacy offers the possibility for interpersonal fulfillment.

By refusing to give prominence to his dream or to allow others any claim over him, Slocum lives without integrity and avoids creating in others an expectation concerning what he will do for or to or with them.

In contrast, Eddie Anderson practices the virtue of fidelity. The midlife struggle of this Elia Kazan character[2] is similar to Slocum's experience; its resolution, however, is quite different.

Anderson has lost all touch with his Greek heritage even to the point of changing his name from Evangelah to Edwin and eventually to Eddie, to satisfy the tempo and life style of the California advertising firm of which he had become an executive. He also betrayed his dream of being a writer by becoming an advertising executive. Marrying a woman who fitted into the dream's betrayal, Anderson

---

2. Elia Kazan, *The Arrangement* (New York: Stein, 1967).

developed friends and a life pattern which almost succeeded in choking to death his dream.

Eddie's story begins just after he has almost killed himself in a car "accident." Even Eddie wonders if it was an accident. As his midlife story unfolds, it reveals example after example of his dream's betrayal. While sexually intimate with a number of women, Eddie is, in reality, emotionally intimate with no one. His writing talents have been twisted into producing advertising copy and glibly soothing the bruised egos of his company's clients. One day, Eddie Anderson "packs it in," and begins the long and painful journey back home to himself. Predictably, his contemporaries are frightened by his actions and view him as being out of his mind. His wife attempts to have him certified as insane, and the family lawyer is sent to "talk some sense into him." The story of Eddie Anderson is really the tale of one man's attempt to return to the spirit of his dream and to rework it, so that he is not tyrannized by its adolescent aspects, but rather revitalized by its life. In his practice of fidelity Anderson gives prominence to his dream and yields to others some claim over himself.

The midlife journeys of these two men, Bobby Slocum and Eddie Anderson, illustrate the following point: the practice of fidelity cannot always be equated with making or keeping commitments. Slocum is committed. He perseveres, but ultimately he is unfaithful to what is unique and life-giving within himself and others. In contrast, Eddie Anderson is faithful to the deepest currents within himself, but in so doing breaks his commitments, and fails to persevere in his original life choices. While Slocum allows his life to become constricted and fearfilled, Anderson deals with the pain and uncertainty of the journey homeward to himself.

This discussion will focus on two necessary aspects of fidelity: prominence of the dream, and yielding to others some claim over oneself. It will investigate the reasons why the practice of fidelity cannot be equated with making or keeping commitments. Perseverance, in other words, is not necessarily a measure of fidelity. Then it will examine why, on the other hand, the breaking of a commitment, in itself, also fails to guarantee that a pattern of growth is taking place.

This discussion will argue that the making and breaking of commitments is not the issue which warrants attention. Rather, a full understanding of fidelity demands attention to two characteristics of the virtue: integrity and intimacy. Living with integrity requires that one follow his/her dream; living with intimacy means that one yields to others some claim over his/her life. These aspects of fidelity will be examined within the context of the adult life cycle. The discussion will conclude with an examination of the question of permanence and with several illustrations of fidelity taken from both present renewal efforts in religious life and from scriptural lessons. Before examining these points in more detail, however, several aspects of commitment, fidelity, and perseverance need investigation in order to clarify the discussion.

WHAT IS A COMMITMENT?

Every commitment involves a choice. These choices determine one's personal, interpersonal, intellectual, religious, and occupational growth. No better way of growing has been found than to "put down roots."[3] Individuals develop their sense of self primarily by choices. A young man, for example, may struggle to decide between a vocation to the priesthood or a career in medicine. In making a choice for one over the other, he establishes a relationship with his choice. A desire to minister to others may be a motivation behind his attraction to these two life styles, but in choosing one, he also decides to develop certain aspects of his personality while neglecting and inhibiting others. On the other hand, he may ideally be able to combine his interests. For most men and women, however, this course of action is just not possible. They must make choices, and over the years try to enhance their lives and realize their potential within the limits of these choices. They must also bear the responsibilities and tolerate the costs entailed by such decisions. People's choices more than anything else individuate and define them.

Every commitment involves a promise. A promise is a particular kind of choice because it describes something that one intends to do in the future. A young woman may, for example, promise to be poor, chaste, and obedient within a particular religious order or congregation. This promise is not a prediction about her future; rather, it is a firm intention. When making this promise, the young woman is not merely describing her present state of mind. She is binding herself to a future course of action. To make a promise is the surest way for individuals to determine the direction of their lives rather than have it set for them.

---

3. John C. Haughey, *Should Anyone Say Forever?* (Garden City, NY: Doubleday, 1975), p. 58.

COMMITMENT AND FREEDOM

At first glance, freedom and commitment appear incompatible. Failure to commit oneself, however, does not necessarily insure greater freedom. Men and women have been led to believe that their degree of happiness in life is directly related to the number of options they have. Conventional wisdom decrees that to increase their freedom, individuals need only to increase their capacity for having their own way. However, this theory is not borne out by experience. George Gilder reports that depression, addiction, disease, disability, loneliness, poverty, and nightmares are the dirty sheets and the unmade mornings of many swinging singles in America.[4]

Freedom has other sides that are critical to any understanding of the relationship between commitment and freedom.

First, freedom can refer to one's capacity to be self-determining. Individuals are free to decide where or with whom or under what circumstances they will "put down roots." In promising to live a particular life style or participate in a relationship, a man or woman freely chooses to grow in one direction and not in another. While it is important to be an adolescent for a while, to explore and to experience different options, it is equally vital not to remain a lifelong adolescent. Individuals continue to explore throughout their life cycles, but perpetual adolescents use exploration to withhold themselves. They dabble in life rather than live it.

---

4. George Gilder, *Naked Nomads* (New York: Quadrangle, 1974).

Second, in making a commitment, freedom is not surrendered. In fact, it may be enhanced by a person's choices. A young man, for example, in committing himself to priesthood may find that his potential for psychological, apostolic, and spiritual growth is greatly enhanced. Possibilities to develop and use his talents increase, his capacity for intimacy may grow, and his relationship with his God can become deeper and more sustaining. Individuals who insist on keeping all of their options open, who refuse to commit themselves, do not necessarily insure intimate relationships, meaningful work, and a sense of personal integrity in their lives.

In summary, by attempting to live one's life without choices and commitments an individual may eventually become unfree. Such a life, without choices, will be determined by outside forces. Commitment, then, is a choice, involves a promise, and is compatible with freedom.

COMMITMENT AND PERSEVERANCE

Today, another aspect of commitment is quite visible: the "breaking" of commitments. Men and women commit themselves to relationships with others, to values, and to God. They attempt to faithfully live out these commitments in a world in which their understanding and experience of themselves, each other, and God grows and changes. In the enthusiasm of young adulthood, men and women often make vows intended to be permanent. However, they cannot always live them out in later years. Sometimes, for example, a relationship dies; sometimes it should be ended. To cling to a commitment solely because it has been promised or vowed, to persevere in it without attending to the destructiveness, rigidity, and lack of life which may accompany this decision, is an exercise in pseudo-commitment rather than of fidelity. Fidelity is exercised in change as well as in stability.[5] There are occasions in which fidelity to oneself, to others, and to God is exercised by acknowledging that a commitment has died.

This thought, however, often frightens us. We do not like change that threatens our life decisions. Witness our anxiety in reaction to recent statistics regarding divorce and resignation from religious and priestly life. In 1974, 980,000 American mariages ended in divorce. That figure is just 20,000 short of one million. In the intervening years, several states have reported that the number of petitions for divorce has outstripped applications for marriage licenses.

In 1975, the National Sisters' Vocation Conference reported that during the previous ten-year period, 30,000 American Catholic religious women withdrew from their congregations.[6] Reasons cited for leaving were: community pressures and life styles, an inability to be oneself within the community, a wish to marry, and a desire for human intimacy.

Furthermore, prior to 1965 the resignation rate among diocean priests in the United States averaged one-tenth of one percent per year, while by 1972 the yearly average was three to four percent. Specifically, the American Roman

5. Evelyn E. Whitehead and James D. Whitehead, *Christian Life Patterns* (Garden City, NY: Doubleday, 1979), pp. 100-106.

6. National Sisters' Vocation Conference, *Women Who Have Left Religious Communities in the United States: A Study in Role Stress, Phase I* (Chicago, IL: National Sisters' Vocation Conference, 1975).

Catholic Church sustained the cumulative loss of over one-eighth of its clergy, approximately 8,000 men, in just six years.[7]

We may react to these statistics with fear, and ask: "Will religious and priestly life as we know it survive?" Such fear will interfere with our ability to examine our own commitments. We need to befriend this fear in order to understand the place of commitment and fidelity in our lives.

Essentially, a commitment should reflect the deepest currents in a man or woman's life; be a path to greater personal, interpersonal, and religious intimacy; and challenge the individual to grow. At times, this is not the case, in both committed relationships and in religious and priestly life. To be more specific, the motivations for an individual's choice to maintain a commitment to a religious or priestly vocation vary widely, as does the ability to deal with the challenge of growth and the stress within the particular vocation. For some men and women, a commitment to religious or priestly life is a reflection of deep and significant aspects of their personality and their life with God. In contrast, religious and priestly life for others may satisfy the need for a life of safety and security. It may be a way for them to cope with sexuality, or provide an outlet for their need to be of service to others. Some men and women may be very dependent upon their congregation or diocese for a sense of identity and a frame of reference.

7. Richard A. Schoenherr and Andrew M. Greeley, "Role Commitment Processes and the American Catholic Priesthood," *American Sociological Review* 39 (1974): 407-26.

In a highly publicized study of American priests, Eugene Kennedy reported that the majority of the men investigated were underdeveloped psychologically.[8] Their identity was related more clearly to their priestly role than to themselves as persons; their vocational choice had been prompted more by factors of status and security than by their interests and abilities; their lives were shaped by the expectations of others rather than by self-discovery. While these men had colleagues and acquaintances, they reported few experiences of intimate friendship. They lacked an understanding of their emotional life, dealt with their feelings through intellectualization and repression, and, while generally successful in their work and their external adjustment, were not fulfilled as persons. They seem to be the Bobby Slocums of religious and priestly life.

Kennedy also reported that a number of priests he interviewed were intent on liberating themselves from emotional and social insularism. While their personal development might have been suspended or delayed through circumstances or personal decisions, they found themselves challenged anew by the problems of growth. They discovered in themselves a sense of purpose and a determination to move forward in their personal development. Common experiences leading to this development were a new job or work assignment, death of a parent, additional education, the effects of Vatican II, a serious failure, and a profound religious or personal experience, particularly with a woman. Kennedy observed that those men who were

---

8. Eugene C. Kennedy and Victor J. Heckler, *The Catholic Priest in the United States: Psychological Investigations* (Washington, DC: United States Catholic Conference, 1972).

more developed psychologically also had a richer spiritual life and a growing relationship with God.

The evidence suggests that maintaining a commitment does not necessarily insure personal, religious, psychological, interpersonal, or spiritual growth. On the other hand, breaking a commitment, in and of itself, also fails to guarantee that a pattern of growth will occur. Clearly, the making and breaking of commitments is not the issue warranting attention. Fidelity, seen as an attempt to live our lives with integrity and the yielding to others of some claim over us, provides more fertile ground for discussion. We will turn now to the first of these two aspects.

FIDELITY, COMMITMENT, AND THE DREAM

Fidelity is a virtue. In old English the word virtue meant an inherent strength, an active quality. The word virtue, for example, was used to characterize the undiminished potency of well-preserved liquors and medicines.

Fidelity struggles continually to overcome the feeling of staleness which threatens any commitment to radical love lived out over time.[9] One element of fidelity is the ability to sustain freely pledged loyalties in spite of the inevitable contradictions of value systems.[10] Two additional components of fidelity are the personal or "dream" aspect and the interpersonal or relational aspect. Importantly, fidelity needs to be affirmed by others. When men and women fail

---

9. Sister Margaret A. Farley, "A Study of the Ethics of Commitment Within the Context of Theories of Human Love and Temporality" (doctoral dissertation, Yale University, 1974).

10. Erik Erikson, *Insight and Responsibility* (New York: W. W. Norton, 1964), p. 125.

to practice the virtue of fidelity, they lose an active or spirited quality in their lives. This loss was Bobby Slocum's dilemma.

Because he failed to develop the personal and interpersonal aspects of his commitments, Slocum ceased to practice the virtue of fidelity. He began to "walk through" his commitments rather than be present to them. Slocum neither gave prominence in his life to his dream nor yielded to others any claim over himself.

This dream is a vague sense of self-in-the-world.[11] Initially, it has the quality of a vague vision and emerges during an individual's adolescent years as an answer to the question, "What shall I do with my adult life?" An individual's dream is his/her personal myth. The youthful dream is filled with illusion. Recall adolescent fantasies of magnificent intellectual or athletic feats; inspiring and sustaining visions of becoming the excellent teacher, the dedicated priest or nurse, the wife-mother in a particular kind of family, the highly respected member of one's community. Adolescents use fantasy to explore ways of being in the world and dreams of the kind of adult life they want to live. At times they may fashion worlds that they can never hope to attain: the would-be hero in pursuit of a noble quest. In young adulthood, the dream is fueled, to a certain extent, by omnipotent fantasies. This situation is necessary, because at this time in life the possibility of accomplishing such a dream is slight. Young adults need to believe that they are greater than they actually are in order to accomplish all that is asked of them by themselves and

---

11. Daniel J. Levinson et al., *The Seasons of a Man's Life* (New York: Alfred Knopf, 1978), p. 91.

others. Growing older, they make choices and commitments, give their dream a definition, and find ways to live it out. In building their lives around their dream during early adult years, men and women give themselves a better chance for personal fulfillment.

In contrast, a betrayal of or an inability to pursue one's dream during a person's twenties gives rise to less desirable consequences. A young woman, for example, may experience a conflict between two life directions: one which expresses her dream, and another which does not. She may be pushed in the latter direction by her parents, by an external constraint such as money, or by aspects of her personality like passivity or a special talent. Thus, this woman may succeed in an occupation or life work which has little interest for her. Her dream remains unconnected to her life; eventually, her motivation and sense of purpose in life simply die.

Initially, many individuals experience difficulty in articulating the specifics of their dream. It sometimes appears to have only tenuous ties to their real lives. The curt judgment, for example, that one's plan is just a "pipe-dream" or the admission that people have succeeded "beyond their wildest dreams" illustrates an individual's difficulty in realistically fleshing out aspects of his/her dream.

In some ways, each dream is similar to that of Martin Luther King in his 1963 "I have a dream" speech. King's dream filled his listeners with a sense of excitement and vitality. When men and women begin to actualize their dream in their lives, the result is much the same. Whatever the nature of an individual's dream, that person has the task of giving it greater definition and finding ways to live it out. Conscious commitments often make the dream more explicit. They are external signs of the internal currents in a man or woman's life.

Betrayal of one's dream leads to an impoverished life, and gives rise to difficulties in later developmental periods of adulthood. Building a life around the dream, however, does not negate the necessity of reworking it into one's life at midlife and during other developmental transitions. During these periods individuals sometimes have to deal with the illusion that the accomplishment of the dream will in and of itself insure their living "happily ever after."

Hence, the dream begins during the adolescent years, builds slowly during the course of an individual's life, and is often made more explicit in conscious commitments. Four factors have an important influence on the development and maturation of an individual's dream: the cycle of adulthood, the midlife transition, personal identity, and mentor relationships.

1. The Dream and the Cycle of Adulthood

The life of an individual develops through a series of alternating stable and transitional periods.[12] The stable periods last six to eight years; the transitional four to five years each. Each stable period has three critical aspects: (1) making certain crucial choices about one's life; (2) beginning to build a particular life structure around these choices; and (3) working to attain particular goals and values within this structure.

In contrast, a transitional period is one in which a person terminates his/her existing life structure and works toward a new one in which to live during the ensuing stable

---

12. Ibid., pp. 49-56.

period. During a transitional period a man or woman's dream emerges for more serious scrutiny. For example, a young man during his adolescent years may have felt a call to religious life. However, after graduation from college and with pressure from his peers and parents he chooses a career in business. While quite successful he feels during his twenties an increasing restlessness. He wonders how to integrate his values into his life structure, and questions his commitments. As he moves into the next transitional period in his life, around age thirty, he will have to evaluate again the commitments he has made and attempt to bring them more into line with his dream.

While this reworking may not result in dramatic life changes, often enough it leads to painful choices. Individuals may have to break a commitment in order to give prominence in their lives to their dream.

2. The Dream at Midlife

The midlife transition is an especially critical time for modifying the dream, primarily because, for the first time in their lives, a man and woman know quite clearly that they are going to die. No longer is death an abstract notion, something that will happen to someone else; it is, rather, an incarnational experience. Physical signs of increasing age; the death of contemporaries; and the growing infirmities and dependence of parents, older relatives, and older priests and community members all conspire to convince the midlifers of their own mortality.

As part of the midlife developmental work, persons must try to understand and evaluate the place of the dream in their lives. Have they lived out the dream, or omitted it from their lives? Some men and women find that they have compromised their dream, or that their pursuit of it is increasingly in conflict with another way of living.

Until midlife, one tends to minimize those aspects of self which are in conflict with the dream. Such action leads to illusions which must be confronted during midlife. Men and women must admit that some of their life goals may actually be in conflict with their dream and that other people are not in the world solely to facilitate the realization of their personal dream.

An individual may be surprised, however, at the insistence and the intensity of the questions that this developmental task of dream evaluation brings. A middle-aged woman, for example, sitting at the dinner table after a long day at work, looking at her disgruntled and complaining teen-aged children, and her tired, balding, and preoccupied husband, should not be surprised that she wonders to herself what her life would have been like if she had not married this man or mothered these children. A middle-aged priest, feeling his own mortality at midlife, might question again whether he made the right choices and life decisions in his earlier years.

Some midlifers feel overwhelmed by the recognized gap between their early ambitions and what they have in fact become. These men and women may console themselves with the thought that if they had only known then what it is they know now, most certainly they would have done it all very differently indeed.

In order to bring personal commitments more into line with the spirit of one's dream, a man or woman must re-evaluate these commitments during each transitional period. This task is a very necessary and normal part of adult development. If individuals are unfaithful to their dream, life will simply close in on them and bring to a halt their growth at personal and interpersonal levels. The demands of duty will rankle more and more, and these men and women will endure these pressures only by encapsulating themselves in an isolated world of their own. They will become distanced observers of what was once an important part of their lives.

As part of the developmental work of the midlife transition men and women must also free themselves from the adolescent tyranny of their dream. While the early dream is rooted, in part, in omnipotent fantasies, the sobered midlifer increasingly grounds the dream in reality. These men and women practice the virtue of fidelity by demythologizing and de-illusioning their dream and by mourning the losses entailed in such a process.

At midlife one realizes that without fidelity to the dream, life lacks genuine purpose and meaning. In contrast, a person's life is enriched to the extent that the dream is given a significant place.

Midlife fidelity, then, includes coming to terms with the gaps, contradictions, and illusions in one's life. The dream will never be realized completely; the hero/heroine will always have flaws; even in success one must accept partial failure. At midlife many men and women are surprised to find that when they no longer feel the need to be remarkable, they are at last able to be themselves. For midlifers practicing fidelity, this discovery is significant. This newly acquired sense of just who they really are and are not ensures that the commitments they make or renew are more truly reflections of the deep inner currents that direct their lives.

3. The Dream and Identity

An individual's dream is closely linked to a personal sense of identity. Whereas the dream can be characterized as the "what shall I do with my adult life?" question, identity is the "who am I?" question. To answer this second query, young men and women must explore their world, experience crises, and make choices. Some identities come cheaply while others are purchased at a great price. Some young individuals, for example, are highly committed but have failed to explore options or to allow themselves the experience of crisis. Hence, rather than achieving a personal sense of identity, they have "foreclosed" their identity. This foreclosure reflects a premature decision about identity, one which allows the adolescent to look away from the contradictions and ambiguities that lie within.

In contrast, men and women who achieve an identity are mature, able to care for others in a nonbinding and noncompulsive manner, and generally are not greatly concerned with personal conflicts. Because they have explored the alternatives available to them, these men and women have attitudes and positions that are not merely a reflection of parental or community norms. Many authority issues are resolved for them, and they need less reassurance from their peers. Even though these men and women will have to rework their identities in response to the changes and developmental crises of their adult years, to a large extent their commitments reflect the inner direction of their lives.

Those who foreclose their identity, on the other hand, are quite "well behaved." However, they also lack independence and curiosity. Their commitments are often externally determined and are not integrated with the inner currents of their lives. It is almost as though they have adopted someone else's dream rather than engage in the struggle to come to know their own. The experience of change in their lives threatens these men and women and seriously challenges their commitments. Because their commitments are often enough the sources of their identity rather than the products of a sense of who they are, these men and women resist any change which might allow them to discover their own personal dream. If they permit themselves the experience of change, crisis, and the discovery of their dream, men and women who have foreclosed their identity may have to change their commitments in order to be faithful to their newfound dream. On the other hand, they may wish to recommit themselves in a new and vibrant way to their original promises after having found that those decisions still reflect the inner direction of their lives.

In summary, individuals who have foreclosed their identity are really "pseudo-committed." This pseudo-commitment can be used to avoid the risk of a personal search and of self-discovery. Pseudo-committed men or women ask the object of their commitment to provide them with an identity and sense of life direction. Many times what looks like the betrayal of a commitment is for the identity-foreclosed man or woman a long overdue withdrawal from an unhealthy pseudo-commitment.[13]

4. The Dream and the Mentor

A mentor assists a young man or woman by facilitating and supporting his/her dream. For young religious and

---

13. Haughey, p. 51.

seminarians, novice or spiritual directors often fill this mentor role. Mentoring is a form of love relationship[14] and a mentor is usually a parent and a peer, not solely one or the other. Mentors may be hosts or guides to young men and women, welcoming them into a new social, religious, ministerial, or intellectual world and acquainting them with its values, customs, and cast of characters. The master teacher, for example, will school the student teacher in the educational folklore and "tricks of the trade," or the pastoral counselling student will be initiated into the world of emotional healing through the supervisor's guidance.

Mentors provide counsel and support in times of stress, or through their own achievements and way of living are exemplars that the young man or woman can admire and seek to emulate. As the mentoring relationship evolves, the young persons benefit by becoming more aware of their dream, gaining a fuller sense of their own authority and their capabilities for autonomous and responsible action. The mentor, then, quite clearly assists the young man or woman in the practice of fidelity.

Formerly, older religious and priests took mentoring as a serious responsibility and thus provided examples of what growth in religious life produced. In this way older priests and religious were able to be a living legacy, and influence the community even as they grew older and less active. The quality of an institution can be judged by the quality of the mentoring taking place within it. Mentoring is a task that needs serious examination within religious and priestly life today as we work toward revitalizing both of these committed life styles.

14. Levinson, p. 100.

5. Summary

One's dream, then, faces a person toward a particular horizon; it points his/her life in a particular direction. When horizons shift, when individuals rework their dream into their lives, new commitments frequently strain former commitments or cause them to be discarded. Ultimately, commitments must be brought into line with one's dream. Eddie Anderson undertook this task so as to be able to live with greater integrity. If we honestly believe that God reveals himself in our history, then the dream is one touchstone to measure our fidelity to God.

One's dream begins in adolescence, and grows and becomes more realistic with the developmental work of each transitional period. The more men and women integrate their dream with their personal sense of identity, and their commitments reflect attributes of their dream, the greater the possibilities for their personal and interpersonal fulfillment. It is always necessary, in fact imperative, that individuals question and reassess their commitments and the relationship of these commitments to their maturing dream. Each person is free to pursue the dream, to ratify and accept it, or to turn away and reject it.

Mentors are guides who facilitate and support one's dream. Befriending, living out, and liberating oneself from the adolescent tyranny of the dream are important tasks for the practice of the virtue of fidelity. There is, however, another aspect of fidelity that needs discussion, the relational or interpersonal component.

INTERPERSONAL ASPECT OF FIDELITY

Men and women do not make decisions about their life commitments in isolation. Commitment is a natural way of expressing both the love that one has for another (the Other) and of proving and preserving that love. Permanence is a property of every commitment that flows from and continues in love. The middle-aged woman mentioned earlier in this discussion, who was having second thoughts about her husband and family, will not necessarily be moved to leave the dinner table, pack a suitcase, and set out in search of a new life. Neither will the religious priest, brother, or sister who seriously questions his/her life commitment decide that a change is necessary. Men and women need to rework aspects of their dream into the reality of their lives. This process may entail changes in commitments or result in a deepening of present commitments.

An individual's relationships are often the most important factor to assist in this reworking process. An ideal preparation for commitment is the experience of intimacy. This experience must be clearly distinguished from the infatuation or "falling in love" experience. Intimacy is real love; infatuation is a step in that direction. Infatuation gives a sense of pseudo-identity, while real love is between real people. Real love means accepting responsibility for one's own happiness or unhappiness; neither expecting another person to make one happy nor blaming the other for one's bad moods, frustrations, or questions about life commitments. A real love relationship takes work and is something into which a person matures.

In reworking one's dream, fidelity requires that individuals consider those to whom they are already committed.

These others have helped one to become what he/she already is; they have assisted with the development and maturation of one's dream. When men or women feel an incompatibility between their dream and their state of life they do not necessarily need to change their state of life. Such a decision may be simple resistance to the pain required for growth. If change in commitment occurs for this reason, individuals will find themselves facing the same difficulties in later commitments as they are in the present one. In other words, they are using a geographical cure to address their unrest rather than practicing fidelity. An examination of the issue of permanent commitments will clarify these points.

PERMANENT COMMITMENTS

While everyone needs to be adolescent for a while, all men and women eventually need to root themselves. Most men and women do not have a problem with commitments, but rather with the idea of permanence. However, there is an intrinsic connection between "forever" and some commitments.[15]

The justification for a permanent commitment is simple: no better soil for human growth has been found. Any commitment, however, that intends permanence but fails to flow from or at least give the promise of leading to love will be a deterrent to real growth. A permanent commitment must always be judged in terms of the fruit it produces. If a man or woman, for example, has become bored, passively indifferent, resentful, and confused in a permanent life commitment, one must wonder what source of life and vitality it provides.

15. Haughey, p. 57.

A permanent commitment appears justified only when the object of one's commitment is consonant with fulfilling the transcendent end that one is capable of attaining.[16] God and other people are the only objects of commitment that seem to qualify for this role. Commitment to institutions, buildings, or ill-defined notions may eventually sap the life from any commitment. People who are fulfilled transcend themselves. The quickest way to get outside of oneself is to make oneself vulnerable to another person.

People express their love for another by saying forever. This word does not, however, mean to persevere "come what may"; rather, it is an aspiration to *become together* "come what may." Forever, then, does not mean fixity. A permanent commitment is not once and forever. Every conscious rechoosing is a renewal of one's original commitment. In other words, the making of a vow does not signify the journey's end, but heralds a journey well begun.

SOME ILLUSTRATIONS

Several of the points developed in this discussion of fidelity can be illustrated with examples of changes in religious life and with gospel events.

Two major aspects of the practice of the virtue of fidelity are: prominence of the dream, and yielding to others some claim over oneself. These two components are quite apparent in religious communities that have historically survived critical periods of change and have entered into a period of community revitalization.

Religious life is a radical following of those conditions set forth by Christ for evangelical discipleship embedded in

---

16. Ibid., p. 59.

a life of prayer and deep faith.[17] However, across the centuries there have been several significant shifts in the dominant image of religious life. These shifts of emphasis have reflected major changes in society and in the Church. Religious life, for example, has evolved over the centuries from the age of the desert, through the ages of monasticism, the mendicant orders, the apostolic orders, to the present age of the teaching congregations.

Each major shift in the dominant image of religious life has been heralded by some significant new foundations which embody the changed image in an especially striking manner. The Franciscans and the Dominicans, for example, divested themselves of landed wealth and thus gave new life to the image of evangelical poverty. Their witness stood in sharp contrast to many of the existing monasteries which had become more like feudal estates. The foundation of these two communities heralded a shift from the age of monasticism to the age of the mendicant orders.

During any transition period some religious orders and congregations go out of existence. The ones that survive manage to blend the new dominant image with their foundation's charism and enter into a period of revitalization. This revitalization is marked by three features: a transforming response to the signs of the times; a reappropriation of the founding charism; and a profound renewal of the life of prayer, faith, and centeredness in Christ.[18]

---

17. Lawrence Cada et al., *Shaping the Coming Age of Religious Life* (New York: Seabury Press, 1979), p. 46.

18. Ibid., pp. 51-76.

In responding to the signs of the times these communities gave to others some claim over themselves. Their renewal was not insular. The founding charism of the community may be characterized as its institutional dream. During each transition period in the life history of the religious community, this institutional dream must be reworked anew into the life of the community. In renewing their life of faith, prayer, and centeredness in Christ, community members support one another in their journey homeward. This journey carries the same attendant risks and possibilities for growth in integrity as the individual's journey homeward to self during adult life.

SCRIPTURAL ILLUSTRATIONS

All three synoptic gospels record the story of a man of great wealth who came to Jesus with the question, "What is still necessary for me to do in order to possess eternal life?" When asked, the man confessed that he had kept all the commandments since his youth. In responding to this young man, the Lord saw beyond his lifelong practice of the law. The man was obedient, but his practice of religion was superficial. Stated another way, he had failed to practice the virtue of fidelity. He was intent on keeping his heart to himself and stockpiling "righteousness points"[19] by observing laws and avoiding trespasses. Jesus spoke to the man's nascent dream and told him that to break through the walls within which he had inured himself he would have to dispense with his great wealth. The rich young man now had the offer of two life directions: one which would speak to his dream, another which would not.

---

19. Haughey, pp. 110-15.

He was asked to commit himself, to manifest externally the internal currents of his dream. He was called on to practice fidelity, to follow the Lord, giving prominence to his dream and yielding to others some claim over himself.

We know well the end of the story. The young man failed to accept the invitation; he remained isolated in his righteousness. He decided against the life, vitality, and risk of his dream, and "he went away sad."

The commitment of Mary, the mother of Jesus, offers another illustration of the practice of the virtue of fidelity. Her commitment underwent a considerable evolution during her lifetime. Mary's commitment was schooled by the Word of God found in the Old Testament scriptures and by the practices of piety and the law taught and lived by her family and the elders of her community. However, she also learned to listen for God's word in places other than the scriptures and tradition. Mary pondered in her heart the Word of God and of men. She also reflected on the events and circumstances of her life.

This dialogue with elements of the internal currents of her life, her dream, readied Mary for the radical change in her commitment which was her response to the annunciation. Though Luke tells us she was "deeply disturbed" by the words of the angel, Mary did not become scandalized that the transcendent and so totally Other Yahweh should become so intimate and immanent. At the annunciation, Mary could not have known what was to be Yahweh's role for her son. She practiced fidelity in that she gave prominence to her dream and, with her "thy will be done to me according to thy word," yielded to Another some claim over her life.

While Mary continued to live within the tenets of Hebrew law and the Word of God in scripture, her commitment was radically transformed. Her life was now a mixture of the old and the new.

It is doubtful that Mary could have been aware of what fidelity would require of her: the maturation of her son; the response to him of church leaders; his condemnation, death, resurrection; Pentecost. She had to shift her horizon of her son's identity from offspring to Lord. No simple feat! Faithfulness would not have come easily for Mary, any more than it does for any man or woman. She could have rejected her dream instead of accepting it and living its uncertainty. Like the rich young man, Mary could have remained isolated in her virtue and refused to yield to another any claim over her.

We have romanticized the life of Mary throughout Church history. She is, however, the image of the Church and of each Christian only because her days were so similar to ours. Mary's life illustrates what fidelity to oneself and to the community can mean in one person's life.

Hope was a central aspect of Mary's fidelity. She lived in hope and entertained great thoughts of what Yahweh would do for the people of God in and through the Messiah. Our commitments will persist if that which we hope for is present in our lives in some measure. A commitment without hope will cease to exist, although its shell may remain. One way for new life to be breathed into dis-spirited commitments is through reworking our dream into them, both individually and communally, so that the hopes that we once entertained have a chance of being revived in our commitments.

CONCLUSION

The Chinese have received credit for an old curse: May you live in an age of transition. It is difficult to answer the question, "What does it mean to 'mean it'?" during any age; at a time of transition like the present one, the problem is enhanced.

The practice of fidelity is difficult, at times even painful. Yet the suffering is no greater than the consequences of betraying one's dream and remaining isolated from others. To question one's commitments is a necessary and natural part of adult life, compatible with the virtue of fidelity. When they risk deepening their commitments, men and women must also accept the possibility that if these promises no longer symbolize the deep directions and currents in their lives, they may have to change their commitments to themselves, to others, and to their God.

Practicing fidelity demands that individuals struggle with the question of who they are, and that they continually rework this question as they face the challenges, relationships, and disappointments in their lives. Existence will have meaning if one's own life has meaning. Fidelity leads men and women to accept their one and only life and the people significant to it as elements that had to be, and that by necessity permitted no substitutions. On the journey of life, individuals need to allow themselves to be mentored and also to mentor others. One must act to insure that the gap which exists between what he/she has become in life and what he/she once dreamt of becoming grows no greater.

Fidelity to one's dream, and nurturing an ability to allow others to make some claim over one's life demands that a person live with passion and vitality; that he/she struggle with intimacy and share the action and peril of the age. The task is difficult, the challenge great. To live without fidelity, however, is ultimately to run the risk of being judged as never having lived at all.

Sister Rita Zeis, S.S.N.D., Ph.D., is a full-time psychotherapist at the House of Affirmation in Webster Groves, Missouri. A member of the School Sisters of Notre Dame, Sister Zeis received her undergraduate education at Webster College, Webster Groves, Missouri; a master's degree in guidance from Saint Louis University, St. Louis, Missouri; and a doctorate in clinical psychology from the Catholic University of America. Sister Zeis did her clinical internship at St. Elizabeth Hospital, Washington, D.C. She has extensive experience in psychological screening of candidates for religious life and in teaching at the collegiate level. Sister Zeis is a member of the American Psychological Association and Psychologists Interested in Religious Issues.

FIDELITY AS PROCESS: BEING AND BECOMING

Rita Zeis

History makes it possible to make different statements in different decades. Not too long ago my title might have been "Unchanging Religious in an Unchanging Church." In the late sixties it was popular to talk and write books about the challenge of change. Some religious changed their appearance; some changed their names. Attitudes changed, too. Life styles have changed so much that it is almost a cultural shock for priests or religious to project themselves back to pre-Vatican days. They rose at the same time, had the same meditation points read for all to meditate on, ate in silence as they listened to table reading, attended Latin Masses, and chanted Latin Office. They were not expected to give their opinions or struggle to dialogue as the community worked toward consensus, or project a personal budget for the year, or decide what kind of government they wanted to have at a local mission, or make suggestions, even decisions, about their ministry or living situation, or to assume the many other individual and community responsibilities religious have today. Vatican II called for extensive changes in our way of life.

Then time passed, and warnings were voiced that all too often external adaptations had far outpaced inner renewal. Individuals more carefully examined their basic spiritual values, attitudes, and commitments to see what kind of religious persons they had become, how their inner selves had changed and developed. Some of them were perhaps surprised to see how much or how little inner change had taken place while they were adapting externally. At some point along the way to renewal, the *process* of spiritual development came to be stressed as well as the product.

Both religious and laypeople have known for a long time that people in our culture who live long enough will pass through infancy, childhood, adolescence, and adulthood. We speak of middle age, and we may have quipped that "Life begins at forty" or claimed when we reached forty that we were arriving at "mature youth." We may have heard about Erikson's crises and Maslow's hierarchy of needs. But Erikson's crises move from adulthood's crisis of generativity versus stagnation to old age's crisis of reacting to one's past life with feelings of integrity or of disgust and despair, with nothing between. If we moved successfully through Maslow's hierarchy of needs, we would be at the top of his hierarchy happily pushing for self-actualization when we reached adulthood, and remain there for the rest of our lives.

IMPORTANCE OF ONGOING FORMATION

In the 1970's the detailed study of adult development came into focus with the work of people like Roger Gould,

David Levinson, and Gail Sheehy. We became more aware that the time between adulthood and the "golden years" is not one long latency period, but rather a time involving exciting and challenging crises and transitions. Now in the 1980's we are very much concerned with *ongoing formation*.

Meanwhile, back at the motherhouse or seminary, before process became popular, clergy and religious were very much into product. They knew what they were to become. They had very specific directions and models. Novice directors and directresses introduced them to the practices of the religious life. The novitiate was a time of intense prayer and solitude, of detachment from the real world. At profession some religious heard the wish, "May you always remain as you were as a novice," implying that they had reached a pinnacle of fervor and were to carefully avoid its loss. After novitiate or seminary training ended, priests, brothers, or sisters went to a parish or mission and did what they could to be "living rules" and to persevere in their vocation.

Now that we are well into the post Vatican II era religious are accustomed to talking about community charisms and personal charisms. They look for ways in which a personal charism corresponds to and can be lived out in the community or religious group. They have become more fully aware of the need to foster integration between the secular and the theological, between personal and community development, and between community living and apostolic service. In the midst of changes in the Church and in vowed life, religious have come to see ongoing formation as permanent renewal, the continuing development of the human person.

A vivid example in my own experience shows how far we have come from the days when members of religious orders were anonymous people who carefully hid their personal identities and made great efforts to avoid being "singular." I remember well a PTA meeting I attended in 1958. One of my first year students had been working diligently to learn what personal information she could about me. The final breakthrough came when a friend of hers worked at the polls with my mother on election day. Now she knew my family name and my mother's political affiliation. The girl's mother, an Irish Catholic and a Democrat, told me jokingly that she found it very hard to see her daughter with such a good friend who was not only left-handed and German, but Republican, too! In those days the girl's learning something about my personal background was quite an achievement.

Today we value the unique gifts and talents with which God has graced us. We praise God for them and strive to develop them. Working toward becoming a whole human person is seen as virtue and a positive goal. Instead of fearing that we will remain at the merely human level, we wonder if we will ever get that far. We understand better what is meant when we are told that on judgment day God just might ask us, "Why didn't you become you?" Because we recognize extensive individual differences among people, we stress inner unity and shared spiritual values rather than external uniformity, and we work for and search out unity in diversity.

PROCESS

Psychologists use the word fixation when they talk about holding on to a behavior which was appropriate at one level of development but which becomes inappropriate as a person matures. Maintaining what is no longer appropriate instead of transforming it into a more mature response will prevent creative integration of the personality and will stunt development. In spiritual development, too, Christians have become attuned to the need to assess their readiness to respond to God's continuing call. They attempt to live out the paschal mystery in their lives, dying to what no longer produces spiritual growth, and rising to new life in the Spirit. Ongoing formation is not just a question of ages and stages, but a movement in faith through the various moments of life, the deaths and resurrections of Christian experience, which make up the lifelong process of development, of being and becoming.

"If there is one thing we have learned during these years of renewal, it is that formation is lifelong. The sense of this lifelong process as being primarily a conscious, continual collaboration which grows toward the maturity of Christ is one of the positive developments of renewal. We have come to learn that we are never fully formed."[1] We have become aware that not merely youth but the whole of life is potentiality, and that we have to accept responsibility, both as individuals and as communities, for the deeply personal process of continued actualization of our potential.

Process can be defined as a continuing development involving many changes. Process, as applied to ongoing formation in the spiritual life, implies becoming and denies the static. "At no point in the life of a religious is it safe to decide to 'stop and preserve what I have' without seriously

---

1. Sacred Congregation for Religious, *Document on Formation* (Draft Copy), p. 1.

jeopardizing the growth process."[2] The Lord spoke rather
harshly of the man who buried his talent instead of using
it. We too are called to use our talent, our potential for
spiritual growth and development.

Individual differences in the process are normal. There
may be periods of fixation or even a regression to less
mature functioning. However, ongoing formation does
suggest a process of integration and internalization of experience, a process which continues throughout life.
Retooling, burnout, changing ministries, second careers,
and increasing options for ministry generally, are elements
of our present reality. They have raised our consciousness
of an increased personal need for awareness of the changes
taking place in ourselves and in the world around us.

Adrian van Kaam alludes to this continuous development when he writes: "The Holy Spirit inspires us to grow
from life form to life form, from grace to grace. Each new
current form of life He leads us to must be a richer, more
mature response in Jesus to the new providential situation
that evokes this response."[3] Being human, we become. In
the course of our becoming, our perspectives and our
horizons evolve.

Buddhist and Hindu societies have always focused on
becoming rather than on *being,* while Western culture has
traditionally put greater stress on personal identity and being than on becoming. Shortly before his death, Thomas

2. Community Life Committee, "Proposal" (Christian
Brothers, St. Louis Province; January 1979): 1.

3. Adrian van Kaam, "Original Calling," *Studies in Formative
Spirituality* 1 (February 1980): 9.

Merton spoke with the Dali Lama, who expressed his concern over the custom of taking final vows, of making a permanent commitment. He saw it as a confining step, and he found it difficult to see the value of promising "just to stick around."

John Haughey likewise refers to the negative reaction some people have to saying "forever." He writes:

> Since "forever" connotes fixity, it is not surprising that many resist committing themselves fully, for it seems to imply that one is making a decision to stop living or growing or becoming. While permanence seems to be a threat to spontaneity, it could and should have the opposite effect. It should foster spontaneity. Once one's life has taken a definitive direction, one should be more, not less, capable of growth. For among other things, people will know where one stands and can begin to relate more deeply to the person. The individual ceases to be ambiguous; he is coming *from* somewhere, so growth for him builds on the strength already accumulated. Since one's life is rooted, growth can be expected, as fruit is expected only from a plant that is rooted.[4]

Before we can so root ourselves by saying forever, we must find ourselves. If I am to be true to myself, I must have achieved an identity, a self to which to be true. Fidelity as process can operate only if I have moved from the role diffusion of adolescence and achieved personal identity. This identity tells me who I am, who I want to become, what I want to keep and what I want to change from both the past and the present. Identity gives direction and focus to life so that I have a core set of values and attitudes I can look to in living out fidelity.

---

4. John C. Haughey, *Should Anyone Say Forever?* (Garden City, NY: Image Books, 1977), p. 63.

However, even with such a core set of values and at
titudes, the vicissitudes of life in this world of accelerating
change continue to challenge Christians and call them to
ongoing renewal so that they can maintain adequate contact with the world around them. For some the necessary
adjustments and change are threatening while others find
the experience a positive one.

SOCIAL IDENTITY

As persons move through the decade from twenty to
thirty years of age, they tend to focus their lives. During
that time an individual first achieves personal, psychological identity and then develops social identity. The current
documents on religious formation are very respectful of
the varying time differences people require to reach social
identity and the decision to make a permanent commitment. Once a final commitment is made, fidelity as process
does not involve a rejection of who an individual has been
and is, but a continued effort to remain aware of personal
development so that new experiences can be integrated
with past ones.

Habits and traditions can provide us with a freeing
security, or they can stifle our growth and development.
Edward Farrell writes:

> Habits, traditions are good. They are like muscles in
> our bodies that enable us to work effectively and easily,
> but if they become calcified they prevent us from work-
> ing and growing. Habits and traditions can become
> blinders and walls that prevent new experience, new
> blood, new thought, new life and energy from reaching
> us. Life styles can become straight jackets, walls,
> prisons; instead of stage camps, they become summits;
> instead of being an entry point to the world, they

become an escape. The tent of the pilgrim becomes the walled fortress.[5]

Farrell emphasizes the need for continued growth when he says: "I am haunted by the first command of Jesus' preaching. Remember what it is? Not 'Pray,' which somehow I once considered the basis of the Gospel. It is, 'Repent,' 'Change,' 'Move,' 'Be converted,' 'Turn around.'"[6] The present day incarnational spirituality continues to call us to ongoing conversion and openness to a changing world.

"Being unfaithful to our own nature, we thereby become unfaithful to God's plan."[7] Whether we talk of human potential or of holiness, this assertion makes good sense. Carl Rogers, in his description of the fully functioning person, further stresses the need for the process of continuing to become oneself. He observes: "I find such a person to be a human being in flow, in process, rather than having achieved some state. Fluid change is central to the picture."[8] Rogers sees this process of healthy living as stretching and growing, realizing more and more one's potentialities and the courage to be. Spiritual development involves being faithful to one's nature and becoming more fully the person God calls one to be.

The vowed life assumes deeper and fuller meaning as it is

---

5. Edward J. Farrell, *Can You Drink This Cup?* (Denville, NJ: Dimension Books, 1978) pp. 76-77.

6. Ibid., p. 81.

7. Arnold Uleyn, *Is It I, Lord?* (Holt, Rinehart and Winston, 1969), p. 141.

8. Carl R. Rogers, *On Becoming a Person* (Boston: Houghton Mifflin, 1961), p. 191.

experienced in daily living over the years. "When we first pronounce our vows there is a sense in which we do not value them—firstly, because we do not know experientially what they will require of us, and secondly, the acquisition of a value requires a life investment. To value requires living that which is valued, practicing it, reflecting on it, and a continuous and consistent converting it as value."[9] This living, practicing, reflecting, and converting which occurs as we live out our vows promotes the continuous development necessary in process.

FIDELITY

In his book *Creative Fidelity* Gabriel Marcel makes a distinction between two different ways of living out a life-long commitment. He notes that some perseverance in commitments takes place at a superficial level with the persons involved dutifully doing what they said they would do. This external performance of promised actions is called constancy by Marcel, and he maintains that mere constancy can actually prevent the development of the persons involved in the commitment. He sees fidelity as involving more than just the performance of promised actions. Fidelity for him involves both constancy and unction of heart. According to Marcel, persons live out fidelity when they preserve the interior sentiments that initially caused them to make a commitment.[10]

Haughey writes at length about the importance of preserving inner motivation if a commitment is to be

---

9. Sister Maureen Fitzpatrick, "A Contemporary Understanding of the Vows," *Review for Religious* 39 (May 1980): 379.

10. Haughey, p. 71.

growth-producing and productive: "All other things being equal, permanence will be a property of every commitment that flows from love and continues in love.... If the loving remains, the permanence of the commitment is assured."[11] Haughey further maintains that any commitment dynamic that intends permanence but does not flow from love and continue in love, or at least give promise of leading to love, will be a deterrent to growth and transcendence. "Concentration on permanence looks at an effect rather than a cause. 'Permanent' is an after-the-fact description of a commitment that has been true to the communion within which it operates."[12]

Our human fidelity is a reflection of and participation in God's fidelity to us. Barbara Albrecht indicates that as creatures of God, created in His image, we are endowed with grace in such a way that we can respond to God's fidelity, His covenant, and give our word on it. "Vowed to God, we live in His fidelity. And this is challenge to and profession of one's own fidelity."[13] She further suggests that it is grace which determines how one is to be person before God, how one makes and keeps vows, and that continuing fidelity to a life according to the counsels demands as much grace as the initial decision and choice. She sees it as necessary for a person to be open to grace and to rely on the grace of God rather than on one's own minimum of strength in the continual effort to remain faithful to the vows. William Hogan also alludes to God's faithfulness

---

11. Ibid., p. 60.

12. Ibid., p. 72.

13. Barbara Albrecht, "Man's Capacity for Final Commitment," *Review for Religious* 37 (March 1978): 207.

when he writes: "Amen comes from the same Hebrew root as the word fidelity, and was meant in its religious significance to evoke the covenant, to recall God's faithfulness on the one hand and the need for our faithfulness on the other."[14]

Priests and religious are called to follow Christ in the service of others. Haughey sees apparent on every page of the gospels that Jesus' commitment is never less than total, while at the same time it is always in process. "He committed himself to do the truth he knew, to live the truth about himself that he was given to see, and to become who he was in his Father's eyes."[15]

For us, as Karl Rahner states:

> The true following of Christ...which is a life with him, consists in allowing the inner structure of His life to work itself out in new and different personal situations....This continuation of the life of Jesus that is new and different for each one of us must be discovered by each individual in the form that is valid for him. The decision that each person must make in order to find his own way of following Christ is itself an act of obedience. It is a listening to the particular imperative of God that put me in my present situation so that I might continue the life of Christ in it; more exactly it is a following of Christ who appeals to my personal freedom and indicates to me my place in His total plan.[16]

---

14. William Hogan, "Faithfulness—Presence," *Review for Religious* 37 (July 1978): 610.

15. Haughey, p. 99.

16. Karl Rahner, *Spiritual Exercises* (New York: Herder and Herder, 1965), pp. 119-20.

Rahner sees freedom as the capacity to create something final, something irrevocable and eternal in response to the call of Christ.

Before Christ left his followers, he spoke of the joy to be found in fidelity. "Remain in my love....I have told you this so that my own joy may be in you and your joy may be complete" (John 15:9,11). In our lives, "everything leads to the surpassing love which the Lord has given us, and which we are allowed to give back to him through the engagement of our whole being for the needs of his love on behalf of the world. This is the love that is the justification for a life in vows."[17] His love frees us to be faithful, to strive toward the fullness of humanity, and to live lives of loving service to others.

SPECIAL CHALLENGES

In some ways clergy and religious face special challenges in this period of history. Luigi Rulla, who has done extensive research on religious vocations, indicates some contemporary problems: "On the one hand, priests and religious are now called to a greater, more challenging social commitment....On the other hand, the same priestly and religious vocations seem to offer less social credit and power, more social opposition or indifference."[18] Among the situational oppositions Rulla sees in the lives of modern priests and religious is the fact that they are called to a life of obedience in a world in which authority is increasingly attacked; invited to live a life of celibacy in a

---

17. Albrecht, p. 212.

18. Luigi Rulla, *Depth Psychology and Vocation* (Chicago: Loyola University Press, 1971), p. 197.

world that continues or increases its cult of hedonism; asked to live a more intense spiritual life when the call to secularization or the use of more available material comforts is present; given more direct responsibility when they may have been formed in a paternalistic environment. Rulla sees the possibility of priests and religious questioning the intrinsic worth of their vocations. He notes that the pressures emerging from today's historical socio-cultural milieu provide a greater personal challenge at a time when there is less social support. He concludes: "Individual responsibility, freedom and initiative are a challenge which the vocationer of Post Vatican II has to meet without the crutches of rigid institutional structures."[19] Loss of supports from without necessitates a stronger, more mature personality structure within.

As our life in Christ becomes more real and solid, and we grow and develop personally, we find that certain things fall by the wayside. Continuity with one's past experiences or decisions cannot be the final criterion for fidelity. Maintaining earlier choices is good only if these choices have produced or give promise of leading to further growth and development. Past experiences can be integrated into our emerging self-picture. As our awareness evolves, a deeper honesty about the past and a more reflective stance to both the past and the present will help us move more confidently into the future. Keeping in touch with our own becoming and the changes occurring around us is essential to fidelity as process.

---

19. Luigi Rulla, Sister Joyce Ridick, and Franco Imoda, *Entering and Leaving Vocation: Intrapsychic Dynamics* (Chicago: Loyola University Press, 1976), p. 263.

Faith is basic to the taking of vows, the making of promises, fidelity. It does take faith to commit ourselves to a future we do not see. Farrell tells us: "Every journey is an Emmaus journey. Manifestations of Jesus are always surprises."[20] Each of us has at times been surprised by the Lord as we have stepped out in faith, as we have heard our unique call to grow from our own base in a given environment. "We are invited to be with Him co-originators of the original divine form of culture, community and personality we are called to be in a given moment of history."[21] Our response to this call is reflected in ongoing conversion, the process of being and becoming. Fidelity as process then is submission to this ongoing conversion of heart which is necessary to be true to one's initial commitment in faith and love.

Faith enables us to respond to God's continuing call in all the varied situations of life. Faith leads us to trust in God's fidelity, His presence with us in every moment of life and growth. Our faithfulness, our fidelity, is a gift from God freeing us to be and to become more personally present to the presence of God in our lives. It further frees us to be present to others.

CONCLUSION

"To believe is to be called beyond where one would ever dare to go; to believe is to know Jesus is with oneself in season and out of season, at low tide and at ebb tide; to have hope and a future....In faith there is movement and development. Each day something is new. To be Christian,

---

20. Farrell, p. 171.

21. Van Kaam, p. 9.

faith has to be new, that is, alive and growing. It cannot be
static, finished, settled."[22]

Fidelity is a process, a being and a becoming. With
fidelity we respond individually, uniquely, to grace. In
order to cooperate with God's grace, we need a continuing
awareness of who we are and of how the Spirit is moving in
our lives. In his farewell discourse, Jesus told the apostles:
"I still have many things to say to you, but they would be
too much for you now. But when the Spirit of truth comes
he will lead you to the complete truth" (John 16:12-13).
Earlier he had said, "If you make my word your home you
will indeed be my disciples; you will learn the truth and the
truth shall make you free" (John 8:32). With gentle sen-
sitivity Christ gradually reveals his freeing truth to each of
us as we become ready to hear it. With fidelity we respond
to his continuing call to follow his way, to know his truth,
and to live his life.

The stress we place on process today is comparatively
new. However, it has been a lived reality in Christianity
over the centuries. Paul said it well:

> Out of his infinite glory, may he give you the power
> through his Spirit for your hidden self to grow strong,
> so that Christ may live in your hearts through faith, and
> then planted in love, and built on love, you will with all
> the saints have strength to grasp the breadth and the
> length, the height and the depth, until knowing the love
> of Christ, which is beyond all knowledge, you are filled
> with the utter fullness of God. Glory be to him whose
> power, working in us, can do infinitely more than we
> can ask or imagine; glory be to him from generation to
> generation in the Church and in Christ Jesus forever
> and ever. Amen (Eph. 3:14-21).

---

22. Farrell, p. 83.

Reverend Bernard J. Bush, S.J., M.A., S.T.M., is director of the House of Affirmation in Montara, California. A member of the California Province of the Society of Jesus who was ordained in 1965, Father Bush studied theology at Regis College, Willowdale, Ontario. He served as student chaplain at the University of San Francisco before assuming the post of spiritual director at the Jesuit theologate in Berkeley, California. From there he went to Boston State Hospital where he interned in pastoral psychology. In 1974 he joined the staff of the House of Affirmation and opened its Boston office. Father Bush has written numerous articles concerning spirituality and social justice, most notably in *The Way*. He has been active in the directed retreat movement and has lectured on Ignatian spirituality, religious life, mental health, and social justice.

"I DO FOR LIFE"

Bernard J. Bush

The title of this chapter is taken from the traditional marriage vow response, where bride and groom pledge commitment and fidelity to one another for life. "For life" means both "until death," and "to the life we will share together." The intention of one who makes such a promise is that it will be enduring and that it will be continually realized in moment to moment and day to day living. Such is the nature of all commitments that one hopes to live out in fidelity.

TIMELY YET DIFFICULT SUBJECT

The difficulty with writing or speaking on the nature of fidelity is that it is such a basic notion. Just as being-as-such is the fundamental concept in metaphysics, so fidelity is a fundamental notion of the moral order. By moral order I mean the interpersonal, the relational, the specifically

69

human realm. Fidelity can only apply to human affairs. Living faithfully means living according to our nature, our human life; that is to say, we live with one another, including and especially with God. Without fidelity and consistency, human life and relationships would break down into utter unpredictability and chaos. In the context of such consistency it is possible for us to live out our lives in wild hope, passionately and fully, in love and in communion with one another. Thus the timeliness of our topic becomes evident. We need constantly to reflect, reaffirm, and in a sense, recreate our convictions, commitments, and values. An unreflective life gradually loses its purpose and direction.

Fidelity is a difficult subject to discuss since there is much in our culture and world that undermines our belief in its possibility. Our culture also makes faithful living difficult. For example, there is a general feeling, amounting to despair, that nothing in human relationships is, can be, or should be permanent. The prevailing mood is "keep your options open." We are told to avoid making irrevocable choices that might bind us later when circumstances have changed. We see a growing reluctance to take stands that might be unpopular or unpleasant, or which go counter to the prevailing wisdom. Much has been said about consumerism and planned obsolescence in our society which affects us all. We are being trained to believe that the grass is always greener on the other side of an endless succession of fences. Unfortunately, we are not being encouraged to cultivate the life we have and to grow in it; rather, we are invited to stay distracted by the "if onlys." There is no lack of voices telling us that if only we had a different job, house, wife, stereo, community, car, body, etc., we would be happy. I am reminded of the scripture passage that speaks of false messiahs offering salvation "over here," "over there," or suggesting, "try this," "try that." We constantly hear that happiness consists of being undecided.

Something about the notion of fidelity is frightening. One aspect seems restrictive, narrow, even fanatical. The word reminds us of our infidelity, our broken promises, and thus stirs up feelings of guilt and unworthiness. When we think of fidelity we may conjure up memories of rules, laws, and customs, rather than persons. We remember the old maxim, "If you keep the rule, the rule will keep you." Some of us are not very happy about where such observance kept us. Thus fidelity means different things to different people, and those meanings are not always positive. Being faithful to commitments and promises can sound very dull compared to the current pressure to live life as a sampler, a consumer of whatever is the latest in fashions, trends, fads.

We do not need to look very far to see evidence of the difficulty people are having with fidelity. The alarming divorce rate, the debasing of life through abortion, drugs, the arms race, global hunger, and pollution of the environment all point to a culture deeply affected by narcissism and superficiality. The decline of the pursuit of excellence causes us to be cautious and wary, expecting to be cheated. A general cynicism pervades political life where people do not mean what they say and do not say what they mean. One's word is, in many cases, no longer one's bond.

God has revealed himself to us as the one who is always faithful to his word. His is the fidelity against which all fidelity is measured and our own infidelity exposed. God

tells us through Jeremiah: "If you could break my covenant with the day and my covenant with the night so that
day and night do not come in their due time, then my covenant with David my servant might also be broken"
(33:19-20).

We are invited to contemplate the steady and faithful
movement of natural events and see the steadfast love of
God in them. However, today it is possible, through the
energy we have harnessed, to stop the sun from setting, to
break God's covenant with the night. How are we to inter-
pret this fact? The arrogant might suggest that since
humanity has wrested control of the evidence of God's
fidelity from him, his faithfulness no longer exists. The
humble among us might say that God has taken an enor-
mous risk by entrusting the earth to us. Perhaps God is inviting humanity to the opportunity for a greater responsibility in collaborating with him. By giving us stew-
ardship over his creation, God enables us to enter into and
to share his creative activity. God may be depending on us
to manifest his fidelity to the world by keeping his covenant with all creation, especially the living and human part
of it. Thus, it seems to me that we are being challenged, in
the face of a fickle and inconstant culture, to reaffirm our
belief in transcendent values and the supreme importance
of human life.

FIDELITY AND FREEDOM

What then are we to say about human freedom? Like
fidelity, freedom is a fundamental fact of human living.
Yet the two seem incompatible and mutually exclusive.
True, as ideas, freedom and fidelity to commitments might

seem contradictory. However, as we live human life, we know that to be truly human means to specify and determine our freedom and our future by acts of choice. Once a choice is made, freedom in that particular respect ceases to be. Our experience teaches us that when we commit ourselves through a choice, we do not restrict our freedom. Rather, we close one door with the expectation that new doors will open and new choices will offer themselves.

The person who puts hand to plow but continually looks back is not a free person. The individual who refuses to make choices and commitments, or who makes them reluctantly, keeping open the option to reconsider them, is a restricted, aimless, inhuman, and ultimately lonely person.

We might consider for a moment the parable of the talents (Matt. 25:14-30). In that story, the man who risked, who used the talents, who took a chance, was rewarded. The fearful, cautious man who dared not commit his talent lost through non-use even that which he appeared to have. There is only an apparent security in non-choosing. The refusal to commit our freedom through making and being faithful to our choices, is, in fact, the stance that takes away even the freedom we thought we had.

CHARACTER DEVELOPMENT

We know that human character is developed by constancy and the successful overcoming of obstacles. We learn that hope is justified when we have persevered through struggle to a successful outcome. All the human virtues and traits that are considered admirable must be developed through adversity. Only through such opposition can we grow in ingenuity, creativity, reliability, loyalty, interdependence, and self-knowledge.

Moreover, the community of humans is absolutely essential if we are going to grow in strength of character. No one can possibly live out alone commitments in fidelity. First of all, we gain our identities and self-knowledge only through the mirroring that significant other persons provide for us. We thus come to know our strengths, talents, abilities, and, equally important, our weaknesses and limitations. Fidelity to our commitments can only exist realistically within the context of accurate self-awareness. It often happens that others are aware of our capabilities before we ourselves are. We need the judgment of people we trust in order to know what we can do. We also need their encouragement and support to carry it out. Much of the trouble people are having with fidelity today stems from a breakdown in community. Where trusted support is absent, living out our commitments faithfully becomes extremely difficult.

Fidelity is a living rather than a static notion. Like basic health, it is something that must be attended to constantly. Just as bodily health can be spoken of as the physical climate in which we live, so fidelity can be considered the moral climate. Our physical health can deteriorate gradually and almost imperceptibly through our neglect or bad habits. We can also improve our health by attention to small matters. Similarly, fidelity is not something that can be taken for granted. Commitments once made need to be reaffirmed and made progressively stronger through careful attention and practice.

RELIGIOUS COMMITMENT

I mentioned earlier that community support is essential to living out our commitments. With the profound changes occurring in religious communities today, many religious and clergy have a feeling of being set adrift. The values once held to be certain and immutable are now questioned and challenged. While there was once consensus and even uniformity in observance, the hallmark of fidelity, now even such a fundamental value as the meaning of the vows themselves seem to be uncertain. There is good and bad in this situation. Perhaps I have been stressing the bad. The good is that we have all been challenged to look deeper into ourselves and into our relationship with God. We need to rediscover in our deepest selves the Spirit speaking to our hearts. Our present situation can be likened to God saying to us: "I care not so much for your formalities, your observances, which have more show than substance; I care about you." Is it not true that in many respects our religious relationships, highly regulated and stylized as they were, had become sterile, formal, and routinized? In the system we lived by and were faithful to, friendships were forbidden. In such a context, how was it possible to live the most important gospel injunction, "Love one another"? I think we did it by changing the word love to charity. However, in language, and certainly in experience, we know the difference between these words. We would much rather be recipients of someone's love than of someone's charity. Paul knew that it was possible to perform heroic acts on behalf of others and still not love them. Perhaps we should reread the first letter to the Corinthians, chapter thirteen, to see that Paul did not put much value on such deeds.

The good part of our situation today, then, is that we have moved from a relatively static and somewhat closed system of observance to one that is dynamic, more open to possibilities, and more challenging to the human spirit. I would like to cite the opening paragraphs of an excellent book, *Mystical Passion: Spirituality For a Bored Society*, by William McNamara. He summons us to live freely and passionately, that is, humanly and spiritually:

> My main purpose is to offer as definite and clear an idea as possible of the meaning, function, and end of passion; and then convince the reader to go ahead and live passionately.
>
> And forever. That's the distinctively human trait— it goes on and on. That's why it is always appropriate to say to a human: "Be yourself," because becoming himself is an ongoing, unending task. This would be a senseless thing to say to a rhinocerous since a rhino has already achieved the quintessence of rhinocerocity.
>
> Human destiny is, in a sense, endless, precisely because it is an exploration into God. The false and fixating sense of "having arrived" or "having finished" is one of the most dehumanizing attitudes of which we are capable. We must be always on the move, always beginning: all over again but into realms of which we are not yet conscious, into Love beyond all our other loves. Our passion must always be mounting.
>
> · · · · · · · · · · · · · · ·
>
> What is important is not vast achievement or triumphant victory, but endless effort. St. Teresa said: "Strive and strive and strive; we were meant for nothing else." That's right. There is such a thing as the triumph of failure—a failure of results. The triumph consists in persevering effort. God sanctifies us through our efforts, not our successes.[1]

---

1. William McNamara, O.C.D., *Mystical Passion: Spirituality For A Bored Society* (New York: Paulist Press, 1977), pp. 1, 9.

IMPLICATIONS OF FIDELITY

Fidelity has many dimensions. Some of them concern the past and some the future, but fidelity is always lived in the present. The aspect of fidelity that concerns the past convinces us of its possibility. We look to history, particularly to salvation history, where God continually reminds us of his fidelity. He calls our attention to his past record, the record of his unfailing *hesed* and *emeth*, his tender and steadfast love and fidelity. In Jesus we have the history of God's incarnate fidelity to us and the return of that fidelity to him. In addition, we have the examples of all those faithful and saintly men and women who embodied the spirit and fidelity of Jesus and lived their lives passionately. The other aspect of the past that requires our attention is our own record of commitments kept and broken. We need to learn about ourselves from our own personal histories so that we can become more and more the good and faithful servants commended by the Lord. This personal reflection is, in my estimation, the true purpose of what we call the examination of conscience.

The aspect of fidelity that looks to the future convinces us of its importance. The fullness of a life of fidelity has not yet come. We live very much in hope, as Paul says: "In hope we were saved. But hope is not hope if its object is seen; how is it possible for one to hope for what he sees? And hoping for what we cannot see means awaiting it with patient endurance" (Rom. 8:24-25).

Since, as I have said, faithful living is a process, we are in movement toward a goal. That goal is supremely important, and hence we are convinced it is worth the effort.

John C. Haughey offers a reflection on hope as it relates to commitments:

> Mary's commitment to Yahweh illustrates what must be true of all interpersonal commitments. They will be lived more in hope than in full possession of what was hoped for when the commitment was made. Commitments persist, even thrive, if what was hoped for is present in some measure. They diminish if nothing that was hoped for is realized. A commitment that is hopeless will cease to be, even though the shell remains for years. One way for new life to be breathed into dispirited commitments is to try to revive the hopes that were once entertained of them.[2]

Later Haughey speaks of the motive that gives strength to commitments:

> Interpersonal commitments that are the product of will power are not ideal. The ideal is that interpersonal commitments be rooted in love and ratified in freedom.
> Some further things could be derived from this position: (1) The purer the commitment the less is it something one makes and the more is it something one yields to. (2) The purer the self-donation, the less one is focused on making a commitment or having made a commitment or even on the commitment itself. One's "eye" is on the one to whom one gives oneself. (3) Commitments that arise from mutual presence are more likely to be persevered in than those whose roots are voluntaristic.[3]

2. John C. Haughey, *Should Anyone Say Forever?* (New York: Doubleday, 1977), pp. 122-23.

3. Ibid., pp. 129-30.

The aspect of fidelity that relates to the present brings both possibility and importance into living reality. The moment in which we now live is the product of our history as well as of our expectations. The choices which constitute the lived now, all we really possess, tell us whether we are faithful or not. Of all the world's societies, I think Alcoholics Anonymous reflects this reality best. Fidelity to sobriety is a minute by minute choice. The memory of past infidelity can be the source of profound self-knowledge. The goal of lifelong sobriety is discouraging and unattainable unless it is scaled down to the single present moment. The example and support of the community of fellow sufferers makes such a goal possible. Similarly, the now of eternal life is present in each moment of fidelity.

This notion and experience of possessing eternal life now would seem like a wild figment of our imaginations if all we had to reflect on was our own fickleness and inconstancy. But we have God's own Spirit within us, the same Holy Spirit that animated Jesus.

THE CHURCH IS THE FAITHFUL SERVANT

We are all members of a visible body which moment by moment proclaims its faithfulness to God. The Church, in the face of a frequently antagonistic culture, urges us to a more interior fidelity. The message is clearly a call to live life. Issues of social justice, international peace, a halt to the arms race, a more equitable economic order, an end to racism and sexism, and respect for life still fall largely on deaf ears. To be faithful to God means to be just stewards of this world he has given us all to share. Our task is no less than to reflect in human relationships and institutions the relationships and fidelity to each other of the persons of the Trinity.

In human form, Jesus is the permanent and irrevocable presence of God's abiding love. Jesus was and continues to be utterly faithful to the Father, inspiring and animating his disciples to be the same. He is the great lover of humans whose will is to gather all of us into the experience of his being and living. We are to "have that mind in us which was in Christ Jesus: his state was divine, yet he did not cling to his equality with God but emptied himself to assume the condition of a slave, and became as men are; and being as all men are, he was humbler yet, even to accepting death, death on a cross!" (Phil. 2:5-8).

We can see then, that fidelity must endure through all obstacles, even death. Without such assurance, death would make a mockery of fidelity. We could rightfully say that if it all ends with death, why bother? The fact, as I have indicated, that fidelity to commitments is constitutive of human life, would probably not be persuasive enough for most of us to live faithfully. Each of us must keep alive the vision and the hope, shown to us by Christ through his Church, that fidelity takes us beyond the current culture. Without this hope, all we have is despair, already present in our popular movements, cults, and psychology. The narcissistic cultivation of *me*, with neither binding commitments nor the atmosphere where love can grow, is essentially bankrupt, and flourishes briefly without rooting deeply.

LOVE, THE STRENGTH OF FIDELITY

Fidelity can easily degenerate into the barren observance of meaningless rules or unproductive commitments. In order to prevent such a zombie-like existence, we must keep alive the love which motivated our commitment by overcoming fear in all its forms. We have many fears. We fear emotional involvement, self-sacrifice, and overcoming the inevitable obstacles that arise. People frequently fear the sustained contact with another that nourishes love. In my work I sometimes hear priests and sisters complain that they do not believe they have the capacity for sustained friendship. They begin relationships over and over again but abandon or break them off at some point. Several such experiences in a person's life can be very demoralizing. Life then becomes a constant series of acquaintances encountered without depth or meaning. When religious or married people call their community or home a hotel, they are referring to these superficial relationships.

It is important to realize that none of us alone can eliminate fear from our lives. It is by sharing fears, naming them and bringing them into the open, that we overcome them. Even the sharing of fear can in itself be an act of courage, hope, and love. The spirit of betrayal and infidelity flourishes when we keep our fears to ourselves and deny their existence through bravado or repression.

The true enemy of fidelity, then, is not defiance or great evil. God sometimes even seems to approve of such passion: "Would that you were hot or cold" (Rev. 3:15). Rather it is apathy, the quiet soul-destroying despair, that makes fidelity difficult or impossible. Infidelity is living in an unconnected state of drift. What someone said about celibacy is similar: the greatest sin against celibacy, the real impurity, is to live life without love.

The love that results in fidelity is a response to invitation, union, and shared life with God and one another.

Such shared life demands that we be true to ourselves and responsible for the choices that make up our personal history. We must be awake and vigilant, using our ingenuity to keep our hope lively. Being faithful in love means living the heart of human existence; that is, being true to our nature and, in Christ, being true to our supernature, since they are now one.

On this matter I would like to quote Joseph Pieper, who in turn cites Johann Goethe and Rollo May in this passage:

> . . . Goethe's well-known lines, "Happy alone/Is the soul who loves" [are] incomparably precise and realistic. Perhaps if we look at the reverse of the coin we will come to a better understanding of this difficult matter. The reverse is the inability to love, fundamental indifference, "the despairing possibility that nothing matters." The true antithesis of love is not hate, but despairing indifference, the feeling that nothing is important.[4]

The reward then of a fidelity grounded in love is happiness and joy: the joy promised us by our Lord when he said, "Well done, good and faithful servant, you have shown you can be faithful in small things. I will trust you with greater; come and join in your master's happiness" (Matt. 25:21, 23). In yet another place he promises, "I have told you this so that my own joy may be in you and your joy be complete" (John 15:11).

---

4. Josef Pieper, *About Love*, tr. Richard and Clara Winston (Chicago: Franciscan Herald Press, 1974), pp. 74-75.

Audrey E. Campbell-Wray, M.A., M.A.S., is ancillary therapies director at the House of Affirmation in Montara, California. In this capacity, she directs the art therapy, spirituality, and activities programs. Ms. Campbell-Wray brings to the staff of the House of Affirmation the richness of her Afro-American culture and a varied educational and experiential background. A native New Yorker, she attended Hunter College before completing a tour of duty with the U.S. Navy as a neuropsychiatric technician. She subsequently received an undergraduate degree in fine arts and psychology from Lone Mountain College, San Francisco; a master's degree in theology from St. John's University, New York; and a master's degree in applied spirituality from the University of San Francisco. Currently Ms. Campbell-Wray is doing doctoral studies in clinical psychology at the Psychological Studies Institute in Palo Alto, California. She is a member of the American Art Therapy Association, the American Society of Group Psychotherapy and Psychodrama, and the International Society of Artists.

FIDELITY AND REMEMBERING

Audrey E. Campbell-Wray

The Promise—A Biblical Injunction—The Lamb

THE LAMB

LITTLE LAMB, who made thee?
Dost thou know who made thee?
Gave thee life, & bid thee feed
By the stream & o'er the mead;
Gave thee clothing of delight,
Softest clothing, wooly, bright;
Gave thee such a tender voice,
Making all the vales rejoice?
   Little lamb, who made thee?
   Dost thou know who made thee?

Little Lamb, I'll tell thee,
Little Lamb, I'll tell thee:
He is called by thy name,
For he calls himself a Lamb.
He is meek, & he is mild;
He became a little child.
I a child, & thou a lamb,
We are called by his name.
Little Lamb, God bless thee!
Little Lamb, God bless thee!

William Blake

God's covenant love is more lasting and more forgiving than all of the goodness of our fellow human beings, and to it he invites your appeal. The Deuteronomic testimony to the fidelity of God implores you to remember how the Lord your God carried you, as a father carries his child, all along your journey until you arrived at this place.

Remember, O Israel, I the Lord, am your God, who brought you out of the land of Egypt.

Remember, O Israel, no other mortals have heard the voice of the living God speaking from the midst of fire, and survived.

"Take care not to forget the Lord who brought you out of the Land of Egypt, that place of slavery."

Remember, O Israel, remember your God when you enter the land, the land your Lord promised to you.

Remember the Lord, your God, when he brings you into cities, fine and large, that you did not build; and fills you with food and goods that you did not grow or make.

Remember, O Israel, in your distress and pain, to return to the Lord, your God, who never forgets the sworn covenant that he made with you.

The Lord never forgets the covenant with all of us who are alive here, this day.

The psalmist learned to appeal to Yahweh, and to accept the simultaneous presence of pain and confidence in love. So in Psalm 119 we hear this prayer:

> Let your kindness come to me, O Lord, your salvation according to your promise....My comfort in my affliction is that your promise gives me life....I entreat you with all my heart, have pity on me according to your promise....Before I was afflicted I went astray, but now I hold to your promise....Let your kindness comfort me, according to your promise to your servants....My eyes strain after your promise; when will you comfort me?...Never will I forget your precepts, for through them you give me life. I am yours; save me, for I have sought your precepts....How sweet to my palate are your promises....My eyes strain after your salvation and your just promise....Steady my footsteps according to your promise, and let no iniquity rule over me....Your promise is very sure, and your servant loves it....Let my supplication reach you; rescue me according to your promise.

Yahweh's response to the promise is fidelity, an embrace. I AM WITH YOU. I AM. It is so simple and so complex.

I AM THE WAY—so I give you my law.

I AM LOVE—so I give you my heart.

I AM SAVIOR—so I give you my Son.

I AM WITH YOU—so I give you my Spirit.

There is nothing you can do to stop God from loving you. God can and will be always entirely faithful and entirely loving. We grow accustomed to responding to outer glitter of one kind or another. We expect to love and be loved only for antecedent perfection. God's love does not depend upon antecedent perfection; it creates the desired goodness in the object loved. We are then able to present ourselves as we are. We are a fellowship of weakness, people processing toward the light. There is a real possibility of standing weakness to weakness, loving one another with God's creative love.

We are a fellowship of weakness.

If I must be perfect before you will love me, then I must be forever unloved.

If I must be perfect before you will befriend me, then I must remain forever lonely.

If I demand perfection of you before I reach out to you, then I have not yet become Christian; and I do not yet understand that to which I have attempted to pledge fidelity.

But weakness to weakness, there is the real possibility that we might love one another and be faithful. This love is not that of antecedent goodness, love that responds only to preconceived perfection. It is the creative love of Yahweh with which we can come as we are, and allow ourselves to be helped and transformed.

The people named ''Without Hope'' must depend upon someone else to set them free from their own hopelessness.

The people called ''Without Hope'' must say: ''We cannot do it ourselves; we cannot heal ourselves; we cannot affirm ourselves; we cannot save ourselves. We cannot remember the Promise.'' They must ask: ''When you come into your Kingdom, will you remember me?" Yahweh's response to the promise is fidelity, an embrace. Come as you are, and let your sisters and your brothers *help you.* Yahweh will give the people called "Without Hope" a new name.

Such are the possibilities of the covenant of faithful love.

> –What was left undone in your youth can now in large measure be done for you by others.
> –Your inner wounds can be surrendered to a process of healing.
> –The battered child in you can be held and comforted by you and by those who love you.
> –The fearful adult in you can try again, holding the hand of a friend.
> –Your tears can flow in the presence of another who cares for you.
> –Someone else had to save us. *Someone else has saved us.*

The possibilities are endless! The promise is remembered in the gentle and mysterious embrace of God's fidelity.

Fidelity to Life—A Social Injunction—The Tyger

THE TYGER

TYGER! Tyger! burning bright
In the forests of the night,
What immortal hand or eye
Could frame thy fearful symmetry?

In what distant deeps or skies
Burnt the fire of thine eyes?
On what wings dare he aspire?
What the hand dare seize the fire?

And what shoulder, & what art,
Could twist the sinews of thy heart?
And when thy heart began to beat,
What dread hand? & what dread feet?

What the hammer? what the chain?
In what furnace was thy brain?
What the anvil? what dread grasp
Dare its deadly terrors clasp?

When the stars threw down their spears,
And water'd heaven with their tears,
Did he smile his work to see?
Did he who made the Lamb make thee?. . .

                                   William Blake

When you stretch out your love and compassion, how far will they go? Whom will they embrace? All of life—some of life—a very tiny morsel? *Where your compassion ends, there your love is arrested.*

We can break the human spirit, and we do. So fragile.
We can survive against the odds, and we do. So strong.

There is only so much battering that the human spirit can take before becoming committed to *death.* Our responsibility to one another is great. Isolation, suicide, war, bigotry, murder, rape, poverty, starvation, control: some forms of death are received, some are given. We see varying degrees of death: defensive armor, commitment to not being touched, neurosis, commitment to the repetition of pain, depression, commitment to inner darkness, numerous unnamed fears of annihilation, commitment to lack of trust. Recognize an unstable inner life, fearful of fragmentation and its own vulnerability: experiencing no place of caring, no place of justice, no peace of life, no freedom.

The child, the lamb, is fragile.

Find your compassion, and be outraged. Rage against the commitment to death. Rage against the arresting of love. Ask yourself: "Where is my love arrested?" At native Americans, Blacks, Latinos, Orientals, Whites? At the waste of woman power, lay power, minority power?

Fidelity to life and to creative love impels outrage at destructiveness, at the incredible potential of nations to blow themselves apart with nuclear weapons, at bombs designed to destroy only people, not property.

Rage against your own destruction and the destruction of the men and women around you. Rage against the destruction of those who dare to love you and are vulnerable to you. Rage against hunger and disease; and against the destruction of the elderly, the handicapped, the angry, the unaffirmed.

The child, the lamb, is fragile. The tiger is fierce.

Fidelity to life is an attachment to a person, an engagement and involvement with a person, an embrace. It allows us to remember the possibility of love and trust and healing.

Do you remember the times when the Lord touched your life? Or the thread of divine presence wove through your years, your trials, your pain? Do you remember your dream? Who you wanted to be, the work you wanted to do, whom you wanted to save, or to whom your compassion poured out? Do you remember your innocent faith and deep, deep longing for oneness?

Yahweh's response to the promise is fidelity, an embrace. The possibility of a life of love is real.

Vincent M. Bilotta III, Ph.D., is a full-time psychotherapist at the House of Affirmation in Whitinsville, Massachusetts, and is chairman of the department of formation ministry at the House. He did his undergraduate work in philosophy and psychology at the College of the Holy Cross, Worcester, and received his master's and doctoral degrees in clinical psychology from Duquesne University. He interned at USAF Wilfred Hall Medical Center in San Antonio, Texas, and served as a staff member at Scott AFB Medical Center in Belleville, Illinois. Here his interests included working in the area of death and dying, training family practice physicians and residents in psychiatry, and dealing with individuals, families, and groups in psychotherapy. In 1976 Dr. Bilotta joined the staff of the House of Affirmation. He is a member of the editorial board of the *Journal of Fundamental Spirituality,* and lectures on formation topics to clergy and religious.

LIVED FIDELITY TO THE SACRED: RESPONDING TO MY HUNGER FOR DEPTH

Vincent M. Bilotta III

The phenomenon of fidelity appears in our everyday life experience in many different ways. For some of us, fidelity means remaining faithful to our commitments, lived pledges and promises. Fidelity for others is associated with loyalty, dependability, perseverance, and dedication. The language of fidelity also includes trust, confidence, reliance, and belief.

Fidelity for many religious means remaining faithful to the rule. Doctors experience themselves as faithful to their patients, teachers are faithful to their students, and parents are faithful to their children. Fidelity can also be experienced in relationship to a cause, a friendship, or a marriage. A daughter who is steadfast in the care of her invalid parent is living out the virtue of fidelity. A faithful Rotarian never misses a Wednesday night meeting. A faithful college alumnus attends all the home football games and contributes each year to the alumni fund. The language of fidelity also appears in the home. The Smith family faithfully eats the evening meal at six o'clock. The children faithfully wash the dishes each evening and place the trash in the garage. As a family unit, they faithfully clean their car each Saturday morning.

In our society we are encouraged to live out fidelity in relationship to ourselves. Thus, fidelity for some is being true to themselves, being their own person. For others, fidelity is being honest with themselves: remaining open to their humanity, aware of their limitations, and claiming their strengths and weaknesses.

On the other hand, the language of fidelity may be lived out as infidelity. Social injustice, abandonment of the elderly, abortions, war, political scandals, all reflect the experience of some people living out a sense of infidelity to others. Preoccupation with possessions, divorce, and self-alienation are variations of the theme of infidelity toward others and self.

FIDELITY IN YAHWEH-ISRAEL RELATIONSHIP

A powerful model of fidelity on which I would like to reflect is captured in Yahweh's relationship to Israel as revealed in sacred scripture. Out of his gratuitous love, God took the unexpected, spontaneous, and direct initiative and invited his chosen people into a life with him. He willed to be present to them and sought communion with them.

Yahweh's fidelity to the Israelites began by reaching out to them and making himself available to them. He shared his presence and made himself known to them. He invited the people of Israel to come to him and promised that in their listening to him with open ears and welcoming hearts, their souls would live.

Scripture shows that Yahweh was everlasting in his fidelity to his people. His mercy endured forever. Yahweh was a good father to the children of Israel. His love for them was stable, firm, compassionate, patient, and dependable. Like a shepherd, he guarded them, stood by them, comforted them, and guided them along his path. For the Israelites, Yahweh was a rock of safety who would be with them always, giving them undying protection and eternally sustaining them. Isaiah described Yahweh as never forgetting the people of Israel, for he had carved them on the palm of his hand (Isa. 49:15-16).[1]

Yahweh's word was integrity itself (Ps. 33:4). His love for the people of Israel was gracious, persistent, and strong. To the Israelites, Yahweh was merciful tenderness and loving kindness. His fidelity was true and steadfast.

The children of Israel responded to Yahweh's fidelity by acknowledging that the world and all living things owe their existence to God and depend on him for their survival and well-being. The Israelites attempted to surrender to Yahweh's process of and presence in creation. As they tried to live constantly in God's sight, they grew in trust

---

1. Scripture quotes are taken from *The Jerusalem Bible*, Readers' Edition (Garden City, NY: Doubleday, 1971).

and faith in him. By practicing fidelity to Yahweh as a faithful wife, the Israelites found their way to God. Their fidelity was rooted in remembering that Yahweh was the Lord, their power and might (Jer. 16:21). Fidelity meant remembering God, turning or returning to him, and walking with him.

As the story of Yahweh's relationship with the Israelites unfolds, we learn how the people of Israel went astray and grew away from intimacy with Yahweh. They lost a sense of the nearness of God and no longer lived constantly in his sight. The children of God forgot about Yahweh (Jer. 2:31) and were no longer inspired by his presence. Preoccupied with their own lives, the Israelites lost touch with the presence of God.

Like an unfaithful and disloyal spouse, the Israelites stubbornly began to follow their own hearts, becoming insensitive and calloused. The children of Israel acted obstinately and refused to give themselves over to the conversion process. They did not listen, but stiffened their necks so that they would not have to hear or receive instructions from Yahweh. Their hearts became hardened, distrustful, and rebellious.

This unfaithful stance of the Israelites led to an impersonal and superficial living out of their covenant with Yahweh. Although they were still specialists in observing the law, this outwardly correct behavior inspired by duty no longer assisted them to know and experience the nearness of God. The constancy of faithfully fulfilled duties no longer fostered intimacy between Yahweh and the Israelites. Walter Eichrodt, an Old Testament theologian, puts it this way: "The merely passive, universal state of submission was not enough.''[2] They needed to be conscious and experientially involved in a deeper relationship with Yahweh.

Salvation history continues as Yahweh invited his people to come back to him out of a yearning to be intimate with him. God asked for a radical transformation of their entire way of life (Jer. 31:31-34). Fidelity must no longer be living by the law in an habitual, routine, external manner only, but it must spring from their deepest selves, as an unreserved surrender. Fidelity means intimacy with God.

Yahweh initiated his people into the deeper implications of fidelity. In order for Israel to find their place with God again, the interior dimensions of their beings had to be uncovered and made ready again to encounter the Lord. The hard scale which had grown over their hearts must be removed.

Fidelity is born in the secret recesses of the heart and therefore springs from the depths of one's being. It expresses the most intimate spiritual dimensions of human beings.

Through the smug confidence of their self-sufficient attitude, the Israelites believed they no longer needed to cling to Yahweh. But God asked them to give up being stubborn and to humble themselves before him. To grow in a new fidelity to Yahweh, the people of Israel needed to purify their hearts and develop a single-minded attention to God's nearness. Yahweh invited his people to see with the eyes of faith his presence in all creation and to surrender

---

2. Walter Eichrodt, *Theology of the Old Testament*, trans. S.A. Baker, vol. 1 (Philadelphia: Westminster Press, 1967), p. 357.

their hearts to the Lord. Through this fidelity of the heart, the Israelites could grow into a vital intimate knowledge of God.

FIDELITY AND SACRED PERSPECTIVE

In order for fidelity to make sense, we must live life with a certain perspective. A faithful person assumes a characteristic attitude which affirms that life has a sacred origin and which believes that there is an absolute reality. Mircea Eliade in his book, *The Sacred and the Profane*, describes this absolute reality as "the sacred which transcends this world but manifests itself in this world, thereby sanctifying it and making it real."[3]

Persons who practice fidelity see that all of life is holy because it flows from God. Sacredness is hidden in the depths of every situation. All of life is precious. Persons who live faithfully are committed to the life of the spirit. They seek to encounter this sacredness in all people, events and things.

Fidelity springs from the innermost core of a person. It is an affair of the heart and not of the head. The more we are centered within ourselves, the better able we are to respond to the deep undercurrents running through our lives. Our hearts respond to the sacred around us. Fidelity is a way of being present to a situation whereby we reach out to encounter its sacredness.

---

3. Mircea Eliade, *The Sacred and the Profane,* trans. W.R. Trask (New York: Harcourt, Brace and World, 1959), p. 202.

DESACRALIZATION: OBSTACLE TO FIDELITY

The possibility of being faithful lies within us all. However, if we live our lives alienated from our interior selves, then the emerging fidelity will become blocked. Living a more profane existence can become a major obstacle to the emergence of fidelity in our lives. When we desacralize our daily living, we become separated from ourselves and from the possibility of fidelity.

As we persevere in habitually fulfilling the duties and obligations of our everyday lives, we may be participating in a desacralizing process. Going through the motions of living, merely adhering to the order of the day, will not necessarily lead us to encounter reality. We may be minimally present to what we are doing, like getting up in the morning but never really awakening throughout the day. Encased in our regular routine, we successfully maintain a spectator's perspective on the everyday. As we observe life but do not participate in it, our senses begin to dry up and remain partially closed. The world no longer reveals its sacred mysteries to us because we are simply not present to what is around us.

INSECURITY AND THE IDEALIZED SELF

As success is more and more sanctified in our culture, the deeper transcendent meanings of reality are lost. We glorify hard work, achievement, and competition; the attitude of the profane takes over and our everyday lives become desacralized. An environment where we are recognized and valued for the quantity of what we do and not for the quality of how we live, becomes an obstacle for the emergence of fidelity.

Since our culture is so highly competitive, the experience of insecurity is always on the horizon of our consciousness. Competition, with its winners and losers, breeds a sense of insecurity in most of us. To fail in competition is to appear weak and incapable, something to be avoided at all costs.

As we dwell on the phenomenon of insecurity, we realize that our culture fosters an idealized image of the person we have to be in order to be accepted.[4] To be weak, to fail, to lose, to be powerless are not valued in our culture. If we appear imperfect, if we seem not to be living up to the ideals of significant others, we experience insecurity. Preoccupied with our insecurity, we lose the sense of the miraculousness of creation, the sacredness of all that is, and the possibility of living a fidelity to the sacred.

We all need to be accepted, loved, and cared for by others. Abraham Maslow points out that in order to continue to grow into wholeness as a human person, we must satisfy our basic needs.[5] If we have had a history of lacking affirmation, security, and need-gratification, we will be forced into a self-conscious and insecure stance towards the world.

In our culture, goodness seems to be equated with doing. If we do well, if we succeed, we are accepted. We all yearn for security, to be rooted in an atmosphere of acceptance. When we do not experience acceptance and affirmation from others, we are driven to seek them.

---

4. Karen Horney, *Neurosis and Human Growth* (New York: W.W. Norton, 1950).

5. Abraham H. Maslow, *Toward A Psychology of Being* (Princeton, NJ: D. Van Nostrand, 1968).

THE IDEALIZED SELF AND FUNCTIONALISM

As a way of coping with insecurity based on the fear of being rejected, disapproved, and not accepted for who we are, we sometimes construct a defense system. Living out an idealized self is a defense structure that helps people cope with the fear of being rejected.

Becoming a self-idealizer is a process by which persons cultivate a false self. They begin to feel that their real self is not acceptable to themselves and others. They imagine that their real self is basically not good enough to be affirmed. Self-idealization fosters a denial and repression of the real self. Persons blind themselves to the real self, disclaiming and abandoning it.

As a result of the self-idealization process, the real self becomes buried and is prevented from growing. The truly human self no longer emerges under the inspiration of the spirit.[6] The self-idealization process paralyzes the integration of the qualities of the real self.

Self-idealizers become caught up in living out a functional mode of presence to themselves, others, and the world. They are interested in producing results. Ultimately they function in an ideal perfectionist manner. Self-idealizers become so caught up in their work of producing perfection that they are blind to other realities. Their only reality is living up to their idealized self-image.

In order to cope with feelings of insecurity and fears of rejection for being perceived as not good enough, self-idealizers may begin to live out a functionalistic attitude towards themselves, others, and the world. They view life

6. Adrian van Kaam, *Dynamics of Spiritual Self-Direction* (Denville, NJ: Dimension Books, 1976).

as a task that must be performed efficiently, quickly, and completely. Life must be managed and controlled in the most pragmatic manner. Work becomes their central value.

Self-idealizers are motivated to live out a functionalistic approach to their everyday existence as a way of hiding their feelings of weakness and insufficiency. Through functionalism, self-idealizers try to escape their shrunken self-image and anxiously search for self-esteem. They attempt to feel more important and self-assured by investing themselves in the doing dimension of reality.

INSENSITIVITY OF SELF-IDEALIZERS

As a way of coping with their infectious insecurity, self-idealizers become lost in the functional tasks of the everyday. They automatically perform the rituals of everyday productive living in a thoughtless, complacent, puppet-like manner. Being task-centered, they try to fit ever greater amounts of work into their everyday activities. As they go through the motions of trying to be very productive, they lose touch with their own presence to self and to others around them. Preoccupied with what is going on externally, they are unable to see and hear what is going on within themselves.

Pulled and absorbed by a functionalistic mentality, self-idealizers have an impersonal approach to reality. They may be aloof, cold, and detached from others. Living their lives controlled by the ideals and rules of others, they pay attention to only the external and superficial. Their activities are performed in an automatic robot-like manner.

As a product of the functionalistic mentality, this impersonal attitude of self-idealizers fosters an insensitivity to their surroundings. Overwhelmed and submerged by the dull routine of doing, they no longer see or respond to the richness and beauty of the ordinary events of everyday. These individuals may find themselves bored by the monotony of doing. Deep within they feel lifeless and uninspired.

Insecurity, the self-idealization process, and the functionalistic mentality all contribute to experiencing in a profane manner whatever is around us. Perceiving people, events, and things in a desacralized way does not allow for the experience of fidelity to emerge. In a desacralized atmosphere, the voice of the sacred in and around us is muffled.

LISTENING TO MY RESTLESSNESS

If I have been caught up in the hecticness of the profane life and my heart has become hardened by the feverish activities of my day, I am still haunted by the voice of the sacred. Amidst the noise of my speediness, aggressiveness, insecurity, power, and cleverness, the sacredness of existence still calls out to me, inviting me to abide in it. Although living in a stance of pride, arrogance, smugness, stubbornness, or complacency impedes deep relationships with people, events, and things around me, the hunger for depth still wells up within me.

Living with a profane attitude towards myself and the world, I distance myself from my deeper self by acting in a hectic manner. Through this hecticness I build defenses in order to continue to feel omnipotent and in control of my world. My hecticness becomes a reaction by which I avoid the call of the spiritual dimension of my life. Yet the inner stirrings of my heart still draw me to a deeper life, the interior life of silence, wonder, mystery, the simple, and the sacred.

I need to listen faithfully to my inner restlessness. The hecticness of my life is part of the unrest due to my lack of someone or something. An inner disquietude permeates my very existence. Hecticness may be a way of fleeing from facing this lack of peace. The more I am involved with the profane, the greater will be the restlessness of my heart.

Symptoms such as body tension and agitated, uncomfortable feelings may indicate that my deeper self is secretly yearning for greater wholeness. Nervousness, uncertainty, and dissatisfaction can be signs that my heart needs something more. I may feel a general sense of deficiency which indicates that I am in need of transcendence.

FIDELITY TO SELF

Caught up in the hecticness of life, we tend to forget ourselves. Profane everydayness conceals the mystery of who we are, and encourages us to abandon our bodies, lulling us into a semiconscious existence. No longer do we live with passion and vitality but rather with passivity and spiritlessness. Desacralization makes it difficult for us to keep our hearts alive as the hearts of children and poets are. It becomes almost impossible for us to taste life. Our real selves are taken for granted; we live our lives in an unquestioning and unreflective manner.

Although we pledge allegiance to God, to country, and to others, thus appearing to be faithful people, our fidelity is unfaithful to ourselves. Intoxicated with enthusiastic activity, doing good for others, we become strangers to ourselves. With no time for silence and solitude, we remain opaque to ourselves and bury deep our unlived lives. As hollow people we remain apathetic, and allow our deeper selves to vegetate.

Thus far, I have alluded to the fact that many people believe that they live out of a sense of fidelity to God and others. However, some of these men and women have unknowingly turned their backs on their own deeper dimensions.

Self-betrayal is an obstacle to fidelity, which is only possible in the light of fidelity to self. But what does fidelity to self mean? To live in fidelity to self means to be aware of ourselves. We are conscious of and familiar with our life experiences. We are attentive to our feelings, our thoughts, and our fantasies. In order to develop an awareness of the many sides of myself, I must remove the blindfolds that prevent me from seeing myself clearly. If I remain entangled in the web of daily routine, I will continue to sleep.

Fidelity to self begins with taking my heart out of the deep freeze and allowing it to thaw so it can be open and receptive to its inner stirrings. As I become aware of the spontaneous reactions within me, I will discover who I am at the moment. Remaining with my experience, I allow my deeper self to reveal who I am.

Formerly my office at the House of Affirmation was on the third floor. After each therapy session I exercised my body by walking up and down the three flights of stairs to do various errands on the first floor. As I listened to my inner stirrings while going over the stairs, I discovered many facets of myself. Some times I would discover myself whistling, feeling happy and free. At other times I would be frustrated, uneasy, or sad. On still other occasions, I would be in touch with fatigue, loneliness, and discouragement. By listening to these feelings, I discovered who I was at the moment.

Fidelity means developing the ability to respond to myself, being responsive to the mysterious dimensions of who I am. I make this response by uncovering how I perceive and relate to the people, events, and things around me. I reveal the mystery of who I am in everything I do. The way I open a door, press an elevator button, eat a meal, walk up a flight of stairs, wash the dishes, brush my teeth, make a bed, drive a car, reach for the salt and pepper shakers, all speak to me about how I am living my life. As I respond to myself, I grow more fully present to myself.

Fidelity to self is also lived out by my attempting to remain faithful to the humanity entrusted to me.[7] As I face my limits and find my place in creation, I answer the call of discovering the self I have been given. In being faithful to who I truly am, I own how powerless I am in light of all that is before me. On the deepest level of my being I feel small and insignificant before this power of life. I become aware of something that is much larger than my little world. I realize that I am not in complete control. The mystery of who I am brings me in touch with my radical incompleteness. On this level of experience I perceive my limits.

Fidelity to self means growing into an intimacy with myself. In order to do this, I must empty myself of my false

---

7. Johannes Metz, *Poverty of Spirit*, trans. J. Drury (New York: Newman Press, 1968), p. 6.

selves and recover my true self. I need to detach myself from all the illusions and pretenses of who I am.

Intimacy with myself originates from the same deeper dimension of myself as the phenomenon of fidelity. Intimacy, like fidelity, emerges from the spiritual core of who I am. Fidelity is a growing into a deeper presence to myself where I am awakened to the sacred mystery that I am. In fidelity I choose to enter into the depth and inwardness of myself and there find the place I belong.

Fidelity is an intimate process of coming home to myself. It is an opening to and an accepting of who I am. In this process I make a home within myself. Fidelity is an inward journey of getting to know myelf. Centered within the home that I have carved out within myself, I grow in at-homeness with all that I am. As I dwell in the interiority of my life, I allow my real self to reveal itself to me. Recollected and ingathered, I can afford to risk being intimate with who I am.

FIDELITY TO OTHERS

Gabriel Marcel states that the more I am able to preserve a sense of intimacy with myself, a sense of recollected, ingathered interiority, the more I will be capable of making real contact with others.[8] Fidelity to others is a returning to my deeper spiritual self. In drawing nearer to myself in the enclosed clearing of my interior self, I am at the same time making it more possible to participate deeply with others.

8. Gabriel Marcel, *Homo Viator*, trans. E. Craufurd (New York: Harper and Row, 1965).

With a firm identity[9] and a strong sense of autonomy,[10] with a well-grounded, secure center for a home, I am able to assume authorship of my life and to welcome others into my intimate space. When I do not have a home, a solid identity of who I am, I find it frightening to give myself to another in intimacy and love.

In being accessible to the interior dimension of my self, I am able to experience true human encounters and dialogues with others. As I remain faithfully in touch with my deeper self, I can implicitly trust others and be open to them. Centered within myself I am able to risk with others and be more vulnerably present to them. Faithfully grounded within myself, I can surrender to others, have faith in them, give credit to them, and accept them as uniquely themselves.

Fidelity to others is being present to them. This being present is a deep, felt, spiritual quality of myself or the other. The presence of anyone is elusive and incomprehensible. To enter into the experience of presence is to open ourselves to the realm of mystery.

When I am present to the other I exhibit my spirit; I radiate my spiritual self to the other. As I wakefully turn toward the other with my whole self, my presence reveals to the other, immediately and unmistakenly, who I am. My being flows out to meet the other. I am ready to make a present of myself to the other. In the presence of the other I let that person be in his/her uniqueness.

---

9. Erik Erikson, *Identity, Youth and Crisis* (New York: W.W. Norton, 1968).

10. R.D. Laing, *The Divided Self* (Baltimore, MD: Penguin Books, 1965).

Fidelity to self means to become fully a person. In order to be fully human I must live with a sense of fidelity to others. We all have a deep need for personal relationships and we must faithfully fulfill this need for people. To be faithful to myself means to stand in the presence of others; in being faithful to others I am faithful to myself.

By this fidelity to others I discover gradually who I am. Being with others awakens me to myself. Sharing the other's presence, I feel more fully human. Participating with others enables me to emerge from myself as the sacred mystery I am. As I am present to the other, the other teaches me who I am. If I listen to the other's feedback of how I am perceived, I can become more knowing of myself. Without the help of others I am unable to find the fullness of which I am capable. Faithfully transcending myself and being present to another, I move along the path to wholeness.

Fidelity to others is living out an attitude of love towards them. In his first letter to the Church of Corinth, we hear Paul urging us to remain faithful to others in love when he says:

> If I have all the eloquence of men or of angels, but speak without love, I am simply a gong booming or a cymbal clashing. If I have the gift of prophecy, understanding all the mysteries there are, and knowing everything, and if I have faith in all its fullness, to move mountains, but am without love, then I am nothing at all. If I give away all that I possess, piece by piece, and if I even let them take my body to burn it, but am without love, it will do me no good whatever.
>
> Love is always patient and kind; it is never jealous; love is never boastful or conceited; it is never rude or

selfish; it does not take offenses, and is not resentful. Love takes no pleasure in other people's sins but delights in the truth; it is always ready to excuse, to trust, to hope, and to endure whatever comes (1 Cor. 13:1-7).

Loving others is to create an atmosphere of respect and reverence for their sacredness. As I affirm their beings, I recognize that we are all precious, fragile, vulnerable.[11] Sharing in our common humanity allows me to become more permeable to others. With my heart softened I am able to listen to the mystery of others.

Fidelity to others means to make room for them in my life. With compassion and gentleness I welcome others into my presence. In order to be hospitable to others I have to abandon and surrender my preoccupation with my need to be in control of all situations. All my childish ways must be put behind me (1 Cor. 13:12). While preparing to be present to others, I let go of my fears and my compulsion to be always perfect and self-sufficient. Emptying myself of my false sense of self, I am able to give my heart to others and become full of presence.

DISCIPLINED PRESENCE TO THE SACRED

In being present to myself and others I gain access to fullness of life, where the transcendent realm of reality is revealed. As I dwell within the deeper dimensions of reality, I encounter the mystery of the sacred.

The ground for the emergence of fidelity is the experience of the sacred. In order to grow in fidelity we must remain in touch with the sacredness of all that is. The path to

---

11. Adrian van Kaam, *Spirituality and the Gentle Life* (Denville, NJ: Dimension Books, 1974).

fidelity is a continual effort to be attentive to the simple appearances of the sacred in our everyday lives. The sacred invites us to participate in its fullness.

We promote the sacred in our lives by cultivating presence to ourselves and others. Fidelity to the deep currents of the sacred flowing within us helps us to remember that we are part of creation, an act of God, and a manifestation of his sacredness. Faithful to the eternal perspective, we discover that our everyday moments reveal various aspects of God's presence. Living fully where we are allows us to go deeper into daily life. As we faithfully probe the surface of everyday reality, we see divine fullness unfolding before us. Gradually our inner urge for the sacred increases.

Fidelity to the holy is being awake to its call and manifestations. Sometimes the signals of the transcendent are hidden by our desire for supremacy and our craving for success, power, and security. Absorbed in a secularized consciousness, we are imprisoned by the very walls that we have built around ourselves, barriers intended to protect us from being hurt.

Our culture has conditioned us to be ashamed of being vulnerable, weak, poor. As a result, we suffer from feelings of inadequacy, inferiority, and insecurity. One of the major themes of the story that we tell about ourselves is that we are simply not good enough. Our everyday hecticness signifies our being on the run. We are trying to escape facing who we are in all of our impoverishment. It is frightening to admit to our shortcomings because we are exposing our vulnerable humanity. In many of our social circles, to be human is not good enough. We are expected to be supermen and superwomen.

In order to grow in fidelity to the presence of God, we must be aware of ourselves, others, and God. Patiently staying with and growing closer to our everyday experience, we allow it to reveal its truths.

Thomas Merton writes about this unfolding of the sacredness of reality when he says:

> Every moment and every event of every man's life on earth plants something in his soul. For just as the wind carries thousands of winged seeds, so each moment brings with it germs of spiritual vitality that come to rest imperceptibly in the minds and wills of men. Most of these unnumbered seeds perish and are lost, because men are not prepared to receive them: for such seeds as these cannot spring up anywhere except in the good soil of freedom, spontaneity and love.[12]

In this description Merton seems to be calling us back to experience what is happening to us in every moment and in every event. He is encouraging us to listen with fidelity to the invisible of our everyday lives, for it is in the invisible, the ordinary, the mundane that the sacred is revealed to us. Within these moments that we usually take for granted, we are being invited to accept the sacred abundance of life.

Through disciplined presence to the everyday we shape our consciousness, raising it to an awareness of God's presence in all that is around us. Through fidelity to the art of disciplined presence we sensitively wait for the sacred mystery of reality to unfold before us in our everyday life experiences.

---

12. Thomas Merton, *New Seeds of Contemplation* (New York: New Directions Press, 1972), p. 14.

LISTENING TO PAUSES

One way we foster our presence to the sacred is by practicing the art of disciplined presence, pausing. Such pausing facilitates an awareness of God in our lives. This simple act of halting for a moment the busy flow of our lives is something that can occur naturally. The stop sign on a corner calls drivers to halt. We pause to catch our breath if we have been over-exerting our bodies. We take time for a moment of relaxation. Before eating we may pause to wash our hands. We stop to take showers and baths, to eat when we are hungry, and to drink when we are thirsty. We halt to get gas for the automobile, pause to do grocery shopping, and take time to mow the lawn or to clean the house.

This practice of pausing recognizes that our lives have a natural flow and our bodies a natural rhythm. Taking breaks is a phenomenon that permeates our everyday lives. Natural pauses occur as we move from one activity to another. We can only read or write so long before we need to take a break from this activity. The commercial during the television program is an intentional break in the flow of the program. After having dinner and lingering at the table to talk further, people may take a break from conversation by moving to the living room. Rising after a night of sleep, we may pause to make our beds and put our rooms in order. All these natural breaks in activities are opportunities to pause.

Breaks in our everyday routine occur naturally and spontaneously, sometimes intentionally. Natural pauses include: getting out of bed in the morning, dressing for the day, opening a door, climbing a flight of stairs, eating and drinking, peeling vegetables and fruits, cleaning our eye-glasses, sitting in a chair, walking from one room to an-other, opening the mail, setting the table. Natural pauses are based on reactions to the flow of the day. The natural pause is the break between one activity and the next. Everyday life is not one long activity but a series of con-nected and related situations. The scene continually changes in our everyday lives. Natural pauses are transi-tions from one scene or activity to another.

Intentional pauses include: taking a walk, listening to music, being quiet and relaxed, taking a vacation or a day off from work, going for a drive in the country, participat-ing in the liturgy, visiting the sick, doing absolutely noth-ing, writing a journal entry, praying, painting the house, waxing the car, planting a garden, reading a book. Inten-tional pauses are breaks in our behavior that are con-sciously willed. They are deliberate, thoughtful responses to the need for distance from everyday routine. We create and cultivate intentional pauses.

Unintentional pauses occur unexpectedly, without plan-ning: being sick in bed, having a toothache or a headache, being in a traffic accident, losing or misplacing something important to us, having a fire on the kitchen stove, dealing with a broken water pipe in the house, experiencing the death of someone close to us, running out of gas on a high-way, spilling a cup of coffee. Such pauses are not willed but simply appear in our everyday lives.

Fidelity to these pauses is most important to the process of remaining faithful to uncovering the sacred in our lives. Listening to our experience as we pause, we take time to practice the art of disciplined presence. Fidelity in attend-ing to these pauses enables us to come home to our center.

Such pauses are occasions to catch a glimpse of ourselves, to remember who we are, and to become more awakened to the dialogue that we are with the world. Fidelity to the pause is an opportunity to avoid being swept away by the swift current of our day's activities. The break in routine is a temporary space to mirror back to ourselves where we are in relationship to God, others, and ourselves.

In our transition from one activity to another, we need to practice the art of focusing back to our interior selves and dwelling there for a moment. Abiding deep within, we come in touch with God's presence in our lives. Fidelity to pauses helps us to grow into a more reflective stance where we allow our realities to reveal themselves to us. By giving ourselves over to each pause and slowing down to see who we are at the moment, we can prevent our sinking deeper into the narrowness of our own preoccupations. From this perspective, fidelity to the pause becomes an opportunity to reorient ourselves and place our realities in the context of all that is. Fidelity to the art of stopping, reflecting, and calling ourselves back to our interior selves prepares the way for an encounter with the sacredness and mystery of life. Living out a fidelity to this sacredness of life, we become more in touch with ourselves, others, and God.

Fidelity to the holiness of all reality is a fundamental dimension of the spiritual life and an essential aspect of growth in wholeness as a person. Fidelity is a call to hallow the everydayness of our lives. We need to become shepherds of the sacred in all creation. A good shepherd is steadfast in love for what has been entrusted to him/her. Fidelity to the sacred means growing into appreciation and love of all that is in my life and in the world.

Sister Kathleen E. Kelley, S.N.D., M.Ed., is director of the House of Affirmation in Webster Groves, Missouri. A member of the Boston Province of the Sisters of Notre Dame de Namur, Sister Kelley received her undergraduate education at Emmanuel College in Boston and did graduate work in counseling at Boston College. Prior to joining the staff of the House of Affirmation, she served on the province administration team and held the position of province personnel director. Before moving to Webster Groves, Sister Kelley did career counseling at the House of Affirmation in Whitinsville. She has lectured extensively in the areas of mental health and the religious life in this country and abroad.

NEVER GROW TIRED OF DOING WHAT IS RIGHT (2 THESS. 3:13)

Kathleen E. Kelley

The subject of fidelity is an intriguing and complex one. In order to sort out the various ways of understanding fidelity, the idea of a "faithful person" comes to my mind as the way we often talk about fidelity.

We are apt to consider fidelity as a response measured by one's behavior. We use terms such as "faithful to duty," "faithful to prayer," "faithful to studies." This understanding implies a consistency of response and a trust that individuals will do what they have done in the past. Such faithful behavior suggests that we can count on those persons because they have behaved faithfully.

However, this consideration of fidelity as a behavioral response does not grasp its essence because negative behavior that flows from a consistent response can hardly be termed "faithful." Examples are abundant if we consider political and military behaviors. Individuals were faithful to duty and carried out their responsibilities, but the end result was chaos and evil. So to consider fidelity as a behavioral response can give an incomplete and confusing picture. When we speak of a faithful person, we presume that one's actions mirror internal values and a mature conscience. Such is not always the reality.

An understanding of fidelity, then, is more fundamental than ascertaining consistent behavioral responses. It seems to me to be best grasped in connection with the most fundamental gift we are given: life.

FIDELITY AND LIFE

At this point in time, our lives have some definition to them. Faith, history, experience, and years have formed them into certain commitments. As we probe our lives, we speak of process, of growth, and of change. We seek fullness of life, integration, human development.

No matter what words we use to try to define life, the basic mandate to live it permeates our endeavor. The words of Jesus offer us hope: "I have come so that they may have life and have it to the full" (John 10:10).

With that promise of abundant life, we have to assume that we have been given the ability to so live it. If we have the responsibility to live, we presume we likewise have the authority and power to do so in a fully human way.

Within the framework of these components of life (authority, power, responsiblity), fidelity has its roots and grows as the guiding force to bring life to abundance.[1]

------

1. These concepts are well developed in an essay entitled "On Becoming Religious" by Mary Daniel Turner, S.N.D. de Namur, in *Starting Points* (Washington, DC: Leadership Conference of Women Religious, 1980).

The proper concept of authority is important for an understanding of fidelity. Most people experience authority as being faithful to someone placed over them. Yet, as with all of life, one has to own authority before giving it over to another. Everyone, by virtue of being human, has authority, understood in the sense that Webster defines it: "to begin or originate anything." We all become in this sense authors of our own lives with the freedom to do with them what we want.

With authority comes both power and responsibility. Power defined as energy or a capacity for action is an important concept today. We speak of power in terms of those who have control over our lives. We use the word in connection with government, corporations. The focus of ministry is on the powerless, those who do not have control over their lives. To realize our power and use it well, starts with the realization of the power within us: the energy; the capacity for action that helps to define us as persons, as men and women, as Christians.

Responsibility comes with power. If we own the power within us, we must use that power for good. Applied to life, these components suggest that individuals have authority to originate their own lives with the energy and capacity to do so responsibily.

The fundamental understanding of fidelity flows from this context. It is the capacity within us to use responsibly our power to author our lives. Power remains a key concept in this definition. The way we use the power given us constitutes our experience of fidelity.

POWER AND BEHAVIOR

Within the human experience there are two major expressions of power: human and divine. The human is seen as constituting the giftedness of what it means to be a person; the divine speaks of the God-life within us. The process of life is to understand the human as an expression of the divine; together they form our personal vision of life.

Fidelity becomes linked to what we perceive as our human and divine lives as lived through history, relationships, and experiences. Fidelity is understood as our fundamental commitment to explore life, both the human and divine, to be faithful to use responsibly our power to author a personal vision of life.

This understanding of fidelity seems clear in the life of Jesus. He was seen as a person of authority who risked using his power to clarify his personal vision. He sought to understand his unique human life and to probe the divine within him. He was driven to know who he was and what the Father was asking of him.

Behaviorally, Jesus was perhaps judged as unfaithful. He was at odds with the religious understandings faithfully held at the time; he broke laws and traditions when the love of persons demanded it. For Jesus it was more vital to be an honest, genuine human being than to be a model Jew. Fidelity for Jesus meant a total immersion in life to discover both his humanity and divinity.

FIDELITY TODAY

What does fidelity mean for us today? The current year has sustained the most human of concerns: life and power. The issues that are debated across our country focus on these concerns: anti-abortion laws; safe disposal of nuclear waste; and the economic feasibility of living. These topics speak of concern for life and the question of who has the power and control.

Life today has great demands made on it. Where to use one's power becomes a problem. In order to explore fidelity to life, we need to explore life itself.

Life has been created with a process of natural growth and flowering. If we plant flower seeds, we expect flowers to grow. We know a kitten will become a cat, a child will develop into an adult.

Life, however, is inserted into an environment which can impact cruelly on it. The environment can deform life, thwart its growth, and cripple it. Yet life is difficult to destroy. Somehow, life of itself demands to be lived. So we see that human beings can endure adversity and mistreatment, yet cling with great tenacity to life.

Yet life is a paradox. Despite its natural flowering, we have to struggle with great courage to foster growth within us. We must work at our authority despite the fact that there is a natural growth process.

This point is where life becomes distinguished as human life. What is characteristically human is the power within us to make decisions. The environment can impact on us, but *we* can impact on the environment.

A further distinguishing characteristic of human life is the quality of uniqueness. No two human beings are identical. As one begins the work of life, personal histories, personal experiences, personal gifts and talents are perceived in a unique way by each individual.

An important component of fidelity to life is the uniqueness that expresses the individual person. Life, seen through an individual's eyes, lived through that individual's actions, is uniquely expressed.

It would seem, then, that we were given a fairly simple task when we were given life. Apparently we should let life flow through us, making responsible decisions which uniquely express who we are as individuals.

But for us life and fidelity to it are lived in the context of a belief system. Our belief system, in itself, is clear and simple. We believe in God. We believe in Jesus Christ. We believe we are to live life knowing, loving, and serving God through love of neighbor and self. Seemingly a simple task to which to be faithful, yet it is a struggle and it is hard work. Believing does not constitute the difficulty so much as living in the human condition with fidelity to those beliefs.[2]

The difficulty for some of us develops when the directives for believing fail to support or enhance our personal vision and experiences. Life, which is meant to flow through us, gets filled with conflicts and tensions. Decision-making becomes paralyzed and uniqueness is sacrificed to conformity. The flow of life gets blocked. People who do not find resonance between their belief system and their experiences simply endure life and exist. They do not involve themselves in living. The essence of life is missing. The faith response is lifeless. Their existence is routine and meaningless.

---

2. The issue of believing and life is discussed at length by Eugene Kennedy in *Believing* (Garden City, NY: Image Books, 1977).

FUNDAMENTAL FIDELITY

Fidelity, fundamentally understood, is that capacity within us as human beings to risk the responsibility of developing our human lives as the unique individuals God has created us to be, and to enflesh our belief systems through that uniqueness.

The most fundamental level of fidelity, then, is focused on our inner life where we accept in honesty the unique human being each of us is and incarnate God's love through that being. Accomplishing this task demands that we reach into the depths of our being to bring alive the capacity to be true to ourselves.

If this fundamental fidelity to life is considered as our primary commitment, it centers our choices as flowing from the life within us. It says that we are taking life seriously and trying to be responsible for that life. This fundamental commitment supersedes any other commitment.

We cannot be faithful to God or to church unless we are first faithful to self. We will not know what faithfulness to another is if we have not responded to the demands to be faithful to ourselves.[3]

Commitment must flow from the ability each of us has to give self at the level of awareness of who we are and who we are becoming. The *first commitment* that an individual has to make is to that life within: to what is possible and essential in order to deserve the name of human being. That dedication is a permanent commitment.

If we make other commitments in life without dealing with this area of growth, we may run into difficulty, con-

---

3. Anthony Padovano, *Free to be Faithful* (Paramus, NJ: Paulist Press, 1972), p. 5.

fusing the demands of these other commitments with the possibility of fidelity to life itself.

Such fidelity to commitment is possible. In fact, it is essential. The need for commitment, to believe in something beyond ourselves, is a profoundly human need. But the possibility of fidelity to secondary commitments is dependent on the fidelity to primary ones.

This commitment to life means that we have accepted the human condition which sometimes makes fierce demands on life. If we have not made that deep commitment to life and resolved to be faithful to it no matter what the cost, we may give up completely on fidelity.

WHAT DOES THIS MEAN?

Being faithful to life means being initially faithful to growth in the truth of who one is. Growth, obviously, means dealing with change. As individuals experience life, they are faced with new data about self. If they have pledged self to the growth of life within, they will struggle to sort out the data and to deal with its truth in their lives. Fidelity comes alive as the driving force to help them find the truth of who they are. This quest for truth will inform their decisions and choices because of their commitment to be faithful to the life within.

As we grow and change, so does our response to life. What remains constant through the changes is the pledge to be faithful to seek the truth of who we are: to clarify identity. Fidelity becomes the base out of which we live, the base of power, determining the use of power through our relationships, our commitments, and our work. We see this truth while at the same time trying to respond out of truth. This inner drive for the truth of who we are, is intimately connected with the life of faith. If we are growing in becoming human we are also struggling to grow in the understanding of God and the knowledge of what he is asking.

To seek the will of God in life becomes a primary part of our search for the truth of identity. Sometimes we may feel that the growth of our own life is in conflict with what we see as the will of God for us. Yet God does not ask anything of human nature that contradicts the divine. In giving us the capacity of fidelity to life, God has affirmed that we can find his will in this life.

DAY BY DAY REALITY

This commitment of fidelity to life is lived out in one arena. Coping with the simple experiences of life is where fidelity meets its greatest test. We can verbalize noble promises, but it is in the encounter with the demands of life that fidelity takes shape. Getting up in the morning, doing household chores, working, relating with people, eating, and sleeping: these activities make up our lives. For the most part, we live in ordinary ways fulfilling ordinary concerns.

The most consistent part of our reality is the time that is today and the demands and activities that fill that time. As days flow into weeks, then months, we somehow accumulate the time that constitutes life. In these ordinary activities we search for meaning and we search for God. We have no other place to look. Fidelity is connected with the way we deal with the day by day realities in our lives. If we face the truth inherent in reality, we are living in fidelity to life.

Reality confronts us with our limits, and challenges us to invest ourselves in it. We are faced with the unreal expectations we have of ourselves, of life, and of others. Avoiding or denying what reality presents to us leads to infidelity. Signs of individuals on the fringe of unreality abound around us: addictive behaviors, workaholism, burnout. If we face the reality of our lives, we touch the fidelity experience. As a result, we will make choices about our lives that are expressive of the truth of who we are, not who we think we should be or who someone else wants us to be. We will try to live as human beings, not as angels. We will risk decisions and make choices that are not always perfect, but which attempt to clarify the truth of who we are. We will trust enough in life to make mistakes and know that life will still go on within us. Finally, we know we will have our share of pain and suffering that will touch the depths of fidelity. Fidelity's most demanding test is in our willingness never to give up the struggle to face ourselves and to live out the truth of that knowledge.

Whenever we move away from being faithful to life as human beings, the signs of infidelity will be present. We will know we have lost our centers. The struggle of life is to keep coming back to that center, for it is the source of the God-life within us, and the place where truth resides.

FIDELITY AND RELATIONSHIP

Our daily lives are a mixture of experiences comprised primarily of relationships. With as much self-knowledge as we possess, we interact with people in experiences, usually through some kind of work.

We do not plunge into life nor are we swept over by it. There is a flow of movement from one direction to the

other and back again. We bring what we know about ourselves into relationships. The experience of the interaction
produces change.

If we are faithful to who we are at each moment in time,
we offer to that relationship our unique response, and
through the interaction grow in the truth of who we are.
This dynamic interaction between self and life applies to all
the types of relationships that constitutes our day by day
reality. Yet, with all the relationships that constitute life,
the self remains the primary relationship.

As a human being that self has a spiritual life, an emotional life, an intellectual life, and a physical life. Within
these dimensions of life are both talents and limitations. If
we are true to this life and have committed the self to
growth, we will responsibly develop those talents and accept those limitations.

As we continue to discover who we are, we come to a
clearer knowledge of what our talents and limitations are.
If we have the capacity to respond in fidelity to that
knowledge, reality becomes a consistent source of truth for
us.

We are who we are, nothing more, nothing less. In essence, we deal directly with the life within us and make efforts to develop all the dimensions of ourselves. Denying
any dimension of life constitutes infidelity and blocks
power.

If we commit our intellectual and physical energies to a
task and ignore its emotional and spiritual aspects, we may
accomplish the work but we have failed ourselves. The
burnout phenomenon is the result. Individuals expend
their physical and psychic energy without accepting their
limitations and acknowledging their own needs. They pour

out life to others and ignore the need to nourish their own inner lives. Some individuals give up the struggle completely. They burn out their capacity for fidelity.

On the emotional level, fidelity means paying attention to the feelings within us that give color and zest to life. They are sources of energy that can motivate us to significant action and growth. If we develop the ability to listen to these feelings and the experiences from which they are coming, we gain a clearer view of who we are. Emotions indicate to us our fears as well as our strengths. They point out to us personal areas that need to be faced in our quest for truth. If we observe these signals, we can more responsibly and honestly invest ourselves in relationship to others. Fidelity to emotions faces us with more truth about ourselves and gives us a sense of our power.

Denial of emotions constitutes infidelity. We are not paying attention to the life within, but more likely are responding to the demands and expectations of life outside.

Fidelity to emotions is an important aspect of fidelity in relationship to others. We learn a great deal about how we feel and think when we come face to face with another human being. We are drawn into relationships with others when we recognize them as touching truth in our lives. If we are honest within ourselves, we will be honest in our relationships. Other people present us with the truth of who we are. If we have committed ourselves to discover that truth, we can risk the pain of involvement with other persons. When we commit ourselves in relationship to another, we are pledging ourselves to honesty, to self, and to the other.

This fidelity is possible because I experience fidelity in another. We cannot know fidelity except through another.

We initially know of the possibility of fidelity through our understanding and experience of God's fidelity to us. Our capacity to be faithful is linked to our ability to perceive God's faithfulness. The experience of human fidelity is a reflection of and participation in God's faithfulness to us. No matter how we may have strayed, we know that God is faithful to us. Such a response of faithfulness to our sinfulness calls forth from us a desire to respond in fidelity.

Fidelity, then, is lived out in a relational context, with self, with God, with others. This relational context calls for a commitment to honesty that is lived out in a congruence between our words and our actions. Practically considered, this principle means that in the day by day living with others, every encounter is marked by honesty. What is said and what is done are expressions and manifestations of an inner fidelity to express the truth of life.

We have all probably experienced conversations where we find ourselves saying things we do not really mean or making statements we do not really believe or promising involvements in projects that are not important to us. We know that when our words do not match our feelings, they ring hollow in our ears. Because of the capacity for fidelity within us, we become alert to those experiences of infidelity.

This experience of infidelity is unique to the individual. It is beyond the realm of another's judgment. What appears as infidelity to another may be for the person involved a courageous decision to be faithful. On the other hand, what seems like faithful living on the behavioral level may be primary infidelity within. We cannot judge. Only the individual in touch with his/her own truth knows.

If we reflect on the experiences of day by day living, we grow in the process of learning greater depths of fidelity. Yet when accompanied by monotony and routine, fidelity is not very exciting. We can easily be seduced away from our center into areas of life that do not draw out the truth of who we are, areas which dissipate our power.

This commitment to fidelity demands a constant investment in reality with its stress and tensions. We are aware of the world, the injustices, the needs. We can dissipate our energies very easily, losing our center of truth. We can grow tired of doing what is right because of outside pressures.

Fidelity to doing what is right in carrying out the prime responsibility to life is arduous; yet, if we lose sight of this priority, we lose touch with fundamental fidelity.

God has entrusted us with life and given us the power to live as human beings. He asks of us fidelity to life because that fidelity allows his life to shine through us enriching the lives of others.

Reverend J. William Huber, Ph.D., is the associate director and a full-time psychotherapist at the House of Affirmation in Webster Groves, Missouri. A priest of the Diocese of Pueblo, Colorado, Father Huber received his undergraduate education at St. Thomas Seminary in Denver. He completed graduate work in marriage counseling at the University of Detroit, and received his doctorate in clinical psychology from the California School of Professional Psychology in San Diego. Prior to joining the staff of the House of Affirmation, he was the founding director of the Pueblo Diocesan Office for Family Life. Father Huber also served in various other pastoral and associate pastor positions before undertaking his graduate studies. He is a member of the American Psychological Association, the American Association of Marriage and Family Therapists, and other professional organizations.

FIDELITY TO THE CHANGING PERSON

J. William Huber

Living out the marriage commitment has been compared to "taking an airplane to Florida for a relaxing vacation in January, and when you get off the plane you find you're in the Swiss Alps."[1] I suspect many a priest and religious experience a similar surprise along their vocational journey. Reality often locates them in places far different from where they had anticipated they would be.

Learning to adapt to the unforeseen future can take its toll. Yet William Lederer and Don Jackson indicate people can make the needed adjustments. "After you buy winter clothes and learn how to ski and learn how to talk a new

---

1. William J. Lederer and Don D. Jackson, M. D., *The Mirages of Marriage* (New York: W. W. Norton, 1968), p. 39.

foreign language, . . . you can have just as good a vacation in the Swiss Alps as you can in Florida. But . . . it's one hell of a surprise. . . ."[2]

This book encompasses ideas on fidelity. It will be good to look at some of the fallacies concerning fidelity as well as some of the truths. Fidelity can mean to be careful in the observance of duty. This definition implies a special loyalty to one's obligations. When fidelity is seen as synonomous to being accurate, then being faithful means responding and living with a mathematical precision, a certain rigidity to one's sense of duty.

This rigidity is the myth many religious and clergy attempt to live out in their commitment to a vowed life. Nothing ever changes for the faithful religious, they maintain. As a result, they view almost all change with skepticism and condemnation. These people have become casualties of Vatican II, their lives and commitments upset by the altering of rules and regulations. Because they believe in a mathematically precise and rigid interpretation of their state in life, they find change disturbing and the life journey confusing as when one deplanes in Switzerland rather than at the expected Florida destination. Many priests and religious appear to have been victims of their own rigid hijacking.

Whenever a decision is based on false expectations, the results are almost certainly doomed to failure. Vocational decisions to marry as well as decisions to live out a religious vocation attest to this truth. The expectation that once a commitment is given, it will endure for one's lifetime can be self-deceiving.

---

2. Ibid.

Despite the well-known figures on the high divorce rate in this country, Americans who marry do not anticipate an eventual divorce. They believe their marriage will be the exception. Candidates for religious life frequently expect that others may not persevere in their calling, but that they themselves will not leave their professed life once they have pronounced their public commitment. They neglect to consider the statistics of post-Vatican II in this area.

Another myth which leads to problems with fidelity is the belief that one's own loneliness will be cured by taking marriage or religious vows. People who marry for companionship soon discover that loneliness is intensified when it is shared with another. In religious life the most intense loneliness is often felt in the midst of one's own community, in a crowd of believers, in a rectory where no concern is shown for being together, in a convent or monastery where all go their separate ways, and persons can be so alone that their death may not be discovered for days.

Still another myth of fidelity is the expectations that one must never question one's commitment, lest such doubts or questioning will cause the loss of one's vocation. Yet, love is a decision, a daily one. Such a decision will not be made with glib facility.

Some people believe that politeness and consideration alone are necessary to make a vocational commitment work. Anger or hurt feelings are not appropriate and should not be voiced. What happens when, despite courtesy and consideration, conflicts arise? When one assumes no conflict will arise if one is faithful, what is to be done when conflict knocks at the door?

CHANGE

Change is at the heart of all living. Every beat of the heart causes a change from its previous state. Only through such change can the heart pump the body's life blood throughout the system. Every breath one takes is made possible only by change: oxygen is exchanged in the lungs for carbon dioxide. Life itself demands change. Only lifeless things do not change of themselves.

Change means a making different, a conversion from one state to another. Changes are built upon the taking of risks. To risk implies above all that we do not know the outcome of our activity. Perhaps that is why persons who are rigid in their fidelity, never see it as a call to growth and to maturity. Persons who do not change will never risk, and do not mature as persons. Ordination and the taking of vows "forever" do not insure instant spiritual or emotional maturity, or even eventual maturity.

"The challenge a person faces is not to see the changeless beneath the change," which is certainly present in all facets of reality; the real challenge is "to accept the change as a real part of the person loved."[3] Only in fairy tales do people live "happily ever after" without changing.

"Fidelity is a commitment to love another person as one is—and since one is a living, growing, changing person . . . a readiness to accept a person no matter how one changes."[4]

------

3. Leonard Bowman, *The Importance of Being Sick* (Wilmington, NC: Consortium Books), p. 89.

4. Ibid.

Sometimes changes come rapidly, as during the early years of life. Most of the time change occurs gradually, almost imperceptibly. According to legend, Milo of Crotona was determined to become the strongest man in the world. He began his training by lifting a calf every day. As the calf grew heavier, Milo's efforts increased and he became stronger. Eventually, he was lifting a mature bull. The basic philosophy behind body building is a slow but steady growth process. Little by little, day by day, faithful practice brings results. Those who want to tone their body or increase/decrease their physical weight or musculature in a few brief sessions, will soon be discouraged by their own unrealistic expectations.

People today use barbells rather than bulls, yet the principle remains the same: a certain fidelity to the changing body. The same theory holds true in one's spiritual life, religious commitment, and/or marital relationship. Sometimes one makes a commitment without realizing it will entail heroic efforts, only to discover later the high cost of fidelity.

FIDELITY TO SELF

Each of us is a changing person. Look at a picture of yourself taken ten or twenty years ago. The religious garb of pre-Vatican II days is no longer the rule but the exception. Society now realizes that religious men and women are as human in their needs as the people they serve.

Our lives as religious have changed in so many different ways: viewing television, going on vacation, visiting home, choosing our work, deciding upon our living situation, being consulted about our future, etc. All these events challenge us to make sense out of this accumulated change.

Not only the externals of our lives have changed. The way we prayed in the novitate or seminary is most likely not the way we pray today. If it is, let us ask: "Why?"

Having experienced such change, we now feel differently. Sometimes the feelings are positive; sometimes they make us uncomfortable. We realize more frequently that we are subject to anger, to love, to strain, to hurt and a hundred other differing feelings that human beings experience. Yet, not so long ago, we believed we did not have such feelings, or if we did, they were bad, and had to be denied or suppressed.

We have likewise changed in our understanding and acceptance of the promises we made on our day of commitment. In our promises and in our vows, we may have committed ourselves to lives of chastity, poverty, obedience, or stability. At the time, we knew intellectually there would be rough days ahead. But none of us foresaw the emotional roller-coaster ride these vows or promises would bring. We were asked to keep the feelings of human love from entering our lives but the feelings came, notwithstanding our promises. Some of us acknowledged and admitted these feelings to our consciousness, and integrated them in a healthy way. Others refused to admit these feelings, and an uneasiness they could not deal with openly crept into their lives. For still others, the feelings were so overwhelming that the individuals withdrew from the priesthood or religious life in pursuit of other lifestyles. For some of these people such an action was good; for others it may have been a form of unhealthy withdrawal. In all these instances, the persons were changing, whether they were becoming more human, permitting their feelings to reach their consciousness, or gaining increasing control and rigid precision in dealing with what they saw as the monster called feelings. People who were faithful to their feelings, openly owned them and admitted them to themselves, at least, have changed for the better. They have become the more human among us who can emphathize with the hurts of others. Like the members of Alcoholics Anonymous who help others, these persons act out of their own experience of hurt and brokenness. On the other hand, those individuals who were not faithful to their feelings, are condemned to lives of anguish and uneasiness, ignorant of what they feel or believing it wrong to feel, yet *feeling* nonetheless. The internal war they wage never ends.

Fidelity to oneself also requires being faithful to the reality in which one finds oneself situated. We do not live in a perfect world, nor is the Body of Christ on earth, the church, perfect. There is no perfect situation, although some situations are eminently better than others. Unfortunately, many religious and priests have attempted to live as though it were possible to be perfect *in this life.* Yet the reward they hope for is limited to the life hereafter. "Be ye perfect as your Heavenly Father is perfect," when taken literally, is a curse rather than the guideline it was meant to be. There is no way you or I can be as perfect as God.

It is true that each of us have been called to a healthy pursuit of excellence. However, we have not been called to strive toward impossible goals that measure our worth by an idealized perfectionism. It is important to recognize that we live in a real world, not in an ideal world. The latter exists only in the mind of God. The ideal world is fantasized in fairy tales. Only immature or emotionally disturbed people expect to live in such a world.

Little wonder that many men and women today are lonely and isolated. They are perfectionists who "fear and anticipate rejection when they are judged as imperfect, [and] they tend to react defensively to criticism."[5] The myth of the perfectionist is that by setting the highest personal standards, one will perform optimally and be totally satisfied. Such people have as their god a critical god, a god of vengeance rather than love and acceptance. Prayer to such a god is difficult if not meaningless. When one expects prayer to be perfect, one can begin to doubt one's faith as well as one's prayer.

Some years ago a young widow in a deep depression came to me seeking help. She was in her thirties and had enjoyed an idealized relationship with her husband until his untimely death. As she recounted her story, I saw that apparently the couple's parents had not shared their idealized views of the marriage. Neither set of inlaws wanted the marriage to take place. Two children and several years later, the marriage actually had brought mutual comfort and companionship to the couple, although not to their parents. One day the couple gave a birthday party for their son. Attempting to make the occasion one of joy rather than of inlaw fighting, a rigid timetable was drawn up. The family was to eat dinner and finish the dishes before the arrival of the grandparents, lest the meal, the undone dishes or the "ill-kept" house become the focus of the party. The young father arrived home from work and the family was sitting down to eat, when the wife innocently remarked that she had forgotten to buy flashcubes for the camera.

---

5. David D. Burns, "The Perfectionist's Script for Self Defeat," *Psychology Today* 14 (November 1980): 37.

Without hesitation, her dedicated husband arose, indicating he would go to the store to purchase the required bulbs. Ten minutes later a telephone call informed the wife that her husband had been in a traffic accident and was hospitalized. Two hours later he was dead.

For two years the widow carried locked within herself many feelings she could not share. She was angry with her husband for ignoring her plea not to leave the table. If he had listened, she thought, he would not be dead. But how could she be angry with one so loving? Instead, by denying her anger toward her husband, she saw herself as a bad wife. She was angry with the inlaws for having placed so much pressure on the couple all their married lives. But why be angry with the parents who had made one's life possible? So she denied her anger, believing she was an ungrateful daughter. Similarly, she was angry with her three-year-old child whose birthday had apparently provided the occasion for her husband's death. But how could she be angry because of the day the child was born? So she bottled up her angry feelings within herself, believing she was a bad mother. Above all, she was angry with God for allowing her husband to die, thus taking him from her. How could God do this? Yet how could she be angry with God, for fear of immediate or certain judgment against herself? So she contained her angry feelings within herself, thinking herself a bad Christian.

In our therapy together, she began gradually to be faithful to her feelings, and to recognize them honestly for what they were. So the young widow began her journey to recovery. Once again she could pray because she could be honest in sharing her anger with God, rather than holding it in. During that period of her life, her anger became her prayer.

This woman's story has its counterpart in the lives of priests and religious, in my experience. Priests or religious can tend to idealize their life styles and vocation, believing they must not become angry or allow others to see that they have feelings. In times past, feelings were looked upon as improper to those seeking the way of perfection in religious life. The "good" religious soon learned to cover up feelings, avoid awareness of them, and deny them outright.

Formation and spiritual directors sometimes encouraged these defenses. Persons who showed emotions such as anger or hurt were considered to be in need of penance, or at least a change of heart. The stoic individual was looked upon as virtuous. Submissiveness was greatly valued while its opposite, assertiveness, was mistakenly considered a vice, even if it was appropriate to the occasion.

As a result, many religious and priests did not learn to be present to the Lord in all their emotionality. To share their anger with God was unthinkable, although it could have been their most valuable prayer. To be assertive with the Lord in stating one's perceived needs was brazen and unheard of. Yet did not David in all his nakedness dance before the ark and Isaiah walk the streets of Jerusalem naked and barefoot for three years? What emotions they displayed, and what emotions they must have caused in others!

In my experience, when one is faithful to one's feelings, negative or uncomfortable as they appear, and shares them with the Lord in prayer, one's prayer life deepens and becomes more genuine and expressive of a real personal relationship with the Lord. Beware the danger of idealizing what prayer should be rather than accepting the reality of one's life.

It is important, as others have pointed out in this book, to be aware of the idealized self and the distinction between what one thinks one should be and what one truly is. To pursue an unrealistic, idealized image of oneself as many religious in the past have attempted to do, is truly to pursue an impossible dream. Little wonder so many people of good will become depressed, lonely, unrealistically guilty, and angry with their lot. They have attempted to pursue an impossible goal: being the "perfect" priest or religious or human being. To accept the evangelical counsel to "be perfect as your Heavenly Father is perfect" as a guideline and an ideal to shape one's life, is far different from believing it to be an immediately obtainable goal. Little wonder such an idealized pursuit of faithfulness has taken its toll on the lives of so many well-intentioned followers of the gospel.

FIDELITY TO OTHERS

Fidelity likewise extends to those around us. Life is an ongoing process and does not conform to any preconceived patterns. While many would see faithfulness to another as being always the same in their regard, never *un*predictable, this attitude idealizes a relationship. "Any relationship has to deal with every situation as it arises."[6] Thus, we are called to be faithful to the *process* of the relationship, to the changing part of the person. "The challenge a person faces is not to see the changeless beneath the

---

6. John J. Collins, "Betrothed in Faithfulness: Symbols of the Covenant," *Chicago Studies* 19 (Spring 1980): 60-61.

change. It is to accept the change as a real part of the person loved."[7] Sometimes, fidelity involves accepting responsibilities for relationships we did not need to enter into or which we have accepted without explicit promises. "A friend can betray his friend by not being present when he is needed even though he has never formally said he would be present. . . ."[8]

In any relationship expectations can be realistic on unrealistic. To feel bound in fidelity to unrealistic, idealistic expectations is nonsense. To know the difference between idealistic and realistic expectations demands a continuing dialogue between the persons involved in the relationship. Without dialogue, there can be no relationship.

Fidelity is a commitment to love another person as that person is: living, growing, changing; and to love the other as the person will become.[9] To pledge your love to another person, human or divine, means to cast oneself into an unknown future that cannot be controlled or predicted. "Fidelity means loving a changing person."[10] It is a readiness to accept persons, ourselves included, no matter how they change. That attitude is the reality of life, not idealized hopes for the future. Only in time does the cost of fidelity become apparent to most of us.

---

7. Bowman, p. 89.

8. Thomas E. Clarke, "Jesuit Commitment—Fraternal Covenant?" *Studies in the Spirituality of Jesuits* 3 (June 1971):74.

9. Bowman, p. 89.

10. Ibid.

Systems Theory takes into account this reality of fidelity.[11] For example, when only one spouse enters into marriage counseling in an effort to change the marriage, or to make it more bearable, the one in counseling frequently tends to mature and to grow beyond the spouse who did not enter the therapeutic contract. When this change occurs, the odds for bettering the marriage are about even. If the spouse not in counseling reacts in a negative manner to changes, the marriage most likely will dissolve. Not a bright prospect for the unhappy, but faithful spouse.

Similar pressures come to bear on religious and priests who, for any reason, enter into therapy. As they grow, or mature, or simply learn how to change their own behavior, the pressures from their community or parish or friends may be so great as to cause much pain to the persons in therapy. Because of misunderstanding the process, observers may expect them to return to their former state, predictable in its unpredictability. The pressure may also be to return as a "perfect, completely whole" person, with no further signs of problematic behavior. Or the pressure may consist of ostracizing the person in therapy now that some

---

11. According to Systems Theory, "the whole is *more* than the sum of its parts. The whole consists of all the parts *plus* the way the parts operate in relation to one another" (Lederer and Jackson, p. 87). Systems Theory is based in part upon industrial and computer technology and had its birth in Einstein's theory of relativity.

As used in counseling, this theory proposes that a constant action-reaction exists between associated people. Feedback is required if the system is to maintain its balance. Unfortunately, feedback is frequently missing, thus creating a troubled relationship lacking equilibrium.

change has occurred and the person's behavior is no longer so predictable.

In all these examples, the community, the parishioners or friends cannot be considered faithful, for fidelity means loving the person who changes in much the same manner as stated in the traditional formula of marriage vows, "for richer, for poorer, in sickness and in health." This fidelity must extend to every aspect of every faithful human relationship.

Although we cannot foresee the future, if we are faithful to the real changes in ourselves and in others, we will continue to mature and grow in our spiritual and emotional well-being. While we may find ourselves in snowy Switzerland rather than in sunny Florida, we will discover that cold-weather life can be just as rewarding as warm, tropical living, provided we are faithful to the changing person.